STEPPING STONES

GOD'S UNFOLDING PLAN OF SALVATION

RITA USHER · MELANIE STORY
AMANDA THORNTON

NEW HOPE®
PUBLISHERS
Gospel-Centered. Missions-Driven.

BIRMINGHAM, ALABAMA

New Hope® Publishers
PO Box 12065
Birmingham, AL 35202-2065
NewHopePublishers.com

New Hope Publishers is a division of WMU®, an international organization that challenges Christian believers to understand and be radically involved in God's mission.

Printed in the United States of America.

New Hope Publishers serves its authors as they express their views, which may not express the views of the publisher.

Library of Congress Product Control Number: 2016906108

ISBN-10: 1-62591-501-2
ISBN-13: 978-1-62591-501-6

N164116 • 0716 • 1M1

DEDICATION

To God the Father, for making me be a branch in the Vine, and for showing me that I cannot produce fruit unless I remain in Him.

To the women of CWJC® for letting me learn alongside them.

To my coauthors, for the privilege of working with them and seeking God together to produce this Bible study.

To my husband, John, for being my spiritual head through it all.

—Rita M. Asher

To "Daddy God," who is always there to rock and hold me, as well as guide and correct me.

To Jesus, my ultimate example in service, humility, and sacrifice.

To my husband, Cliff, who has been by my side through every mountain and every valley, and who is everything I am not: patient, calm, and fun.

To my children: Morgan, Alli Grace, Amelia, and Travis, who have each taught me so much about how God sees us, how I should see others, and how important it is to be in the Word daily. God is always good!

To my coauthors—Rita, you have been the one continuing thread through this whole journey, and you have taught me to dig deeper into God's Word and to cover everything in prayer.

To the women of CWJC, who have inspired me to take a fresh look at God's Word and to look for what we need to know.

—Melanie A. Story

To God Almighty, Your name is Jehovah, the creator of the universe; *Elohim*, most merciful, I praise You in all the earth! Without You, Father, I would be nothing. You are the only One who truly knows me, and pours out Your mercy and grace by giving us Your precious Son, Jesus, on the Cross. I thank You for Your Holy Spirit's writing and guiding this work.

"When I consider Your heavens, the work of Your fingers, the moon and the stars, which You have ordained, what is man that You are mindful of him, and the son of man that You visit him? For You have made him a little lower than the angels, and You have crowned him with glory and honor" (Psalm 8:3–5 NKJV).

My husband, Robert, thank you for inspiring me to become the woman of God I was meant to be all along.

My children, Caralise and Caleb, thank you for inspiring me to laugh and appreciate each and every blessing (every good and perfect gift is from above).

4

First Baptist Church Starkville, the Golden Triangle Baptist Association, and Rev. Dan Robertson, Rev. Chip Stevens, and Mrs. Pat Belcher, thank you for helping me grow in my faith and in prayer; and thank you for supporting and pursuing God's plan for the CWJC and CMJC® ministry.

The women of CWJC, thank you, my sisters, for supporting one another through prayer and encouragement. You have been my spiritual family.

—Amanda H. Thornton

ACKNOWLEDGMENTS

Studying through the years, we have collected cross-references and absorbed teaching from many sources that would be impossible to properly credit. Where essential, we have credited sources in these lesson studies, however, there have been many influences on our understanding of the Bible. For almost 30 years, Rita has taught adult Sunday School, and materials provided by the Southern Baptist Convention (*Explore the Bible*, and others) influenced and have helped in the preparation of these lessons. *The Bible Exposition Commentary* by William Wiersbe, as well as *Commentary Critical and Explanatory on the Whole Bible* by Rev. Robert Jamieson, DD; Rev. A. R. Fausset, A. M.; and Rev. David Brown, DD, are outstanding references.

We owe these sources a debt of gratitude for what they have added to our study, and now your study, of God's Word with your groups.

5

CONTENTS

PREFACE

"Truly he is my rock and my salvation; he is my fortress,
I will not be shaken."
—PSALM 62:6

If you were to search for *rock* in the Bible, you might find more than 100 definitions. Here, *rock* represents the essence of a relationship with God: an unfailing strength and shelter.

As you read and study the Bible, take note of God's character and His nature. Follow His steps throughout this journey and allow each lesson to become a stepping stone, building to the next. Step by step, these lessons reveal the mighty hand of God, drawing people into His presence and guiding each one of us toward salvation. From the beginning of the Bible to the end, He's been leading mankind toward salvation, guiding us into a deeper understanding of who He is and His purpose for mankind.

Ask the question, "What does a person need to know to be saved?" and consider your answer. After reading each lesson, reflect upon the stepping stones that God has positioned. From the Old Testament to the New Testament, He's leading people toward the opportunity for a relationship with the Chief Cornerstone, Jesus Christ.

Exodus 17:6

> *"'I will stand there before you by the rock at Horeb. Strike the rock, and water will come out of it for the people to drink.' So Moses did this in the sight of the elders of Israel."*

Exodus 33:21–23

> *"Then the LORD said, 'There is a place near me where you may stand on a rock. When my glory passes by, I will put you in a cleft in the rock and cover you with my hand until I have passed by. Then I will remove my hand and you will see my back; but my face must not be seen.'"*

Psalm 78:35

> *"They remembered that God was their Rock, that God Most High was their Redeemer."*

Matthew 7:25

> *"The rain came down, the streams rose, and the winds blew and beat against that house; yet it did not fall, because it had its foundation on the rock."*

1 Corinthians 10:3–4

> *"They all ate the same spiritual food and drank the same spiritual drink; for they drank from the spiritual rock that accompanied them, and that rock was Christ."*

Ephesians 2:19–20

> *"Consequently, you are no longer foreigners and strangers, but fellow citizens with God's people and also members of his household, built on the foundation of the apostles and prophets, with Christ Jesus himself as the chief cornerstone."*

Understand that God has been leading us all along, from the Old Testament through the New Testament toward the Chief Cornerstone, Jesus Christ.

LETTER TO TEACHERS

Dear Teacher of the Word,

Welcome to *Stepping Stones: God's Unfolding Plan of Salvation*. Many people know stories from the Bible. We know about Adam and Eve and the snake. We know about Father Abraham and his many descendants. We know the story of Joseph and his coat of many colors. We have heard about David and Bathsheba, and Solomon. We probably celebrate the biblical events of baby Jesus in the manger and Jesus rising from the dead. But many don't see how the stories, the biblical events and peoples, relate to one another and how they form a bigger picture of what God has done for mankind. Many people, even people who attend church regularly or who are good students of the Word, need to realize that the Bible is more than a collection of stories; it is *one* story—about God's redemption of humanity.

This Bible study shows God's unfolding plan of salvation.

In *Stepping Stones*, we begin with Creation, when God created man and woman for relationship with God, and placed them in a beautiful garden. Then something went wrong. The man and woman disobeyed God—sinning against God and breaking the relationship between God and mankind. Yet, even in this story of the Fall, there is hope. God promised a Savior, a way to restore mankind's relationship with Him.

In a later generation, God calls Abram and promises to make him a blessing to the whole world. Here God begins to work in one family and through their lineage will bring forth the promised Savior. The rest of the Bible stories are about how God keeps all of His promises. It is called a progressive revelation because, with each Bible passage, God reveals more about Himself, about the coming Savior, and about mankind—us.

One of the goals of this Bible study is to help individuals see what God was doing, as recorded in the Old Testament: how He prepared mankind for the Savior through promises, and through visual pictures He provided for us, such as those of the Passover.

Then *Stepping Stones* focuses on Jesus and shows how He fulfills all that God prepared beforehand. We look at Jesus' life and character and at His sacrifice on the Cross, which was principal among the reasons that God's Son came into this world. This study culminates in a gospel presentation, because it is not enough to simply know these facts. The story God is telling through His Word calls for response.

Stepping Stones will conclude study with two lessons that show how the gospel changed the lives of two very different people, the Apostle Peter and the Apostle Paul. The goal of *Stepping Stones* is changed lives.

How *Stepping Stones* Bible Study came to be:

Stepping Stones Bible study was written originally for use at Christian Women's Job Corps® in Golden Triangle, Mississippi. People from diverse church backgrounds, from the unsaved to the wives of pastors, gathered to study together.

These lessons have been well received by the CWJC® participants. We have heard many comments, such as, "I came for the CWJC® computer training, but *the Bible study. . . !*" Participants have expressed repeatedly that studying the Bible from beginning to end opened their eyes to truth—truths they had never known—and that they can now see the bigger picture.

What *Stepping Stones* Bible Study includes:

Scholars have written about biblical events for thousands of years. How to decide what to include here? Answer: What a person needs to know to receive salvation. We agree with the Apostle Paul:

> "When I came to you, brothers, I did not come with eloquence or superior wisdom as I proclaimed to you the testimony about God. For I resolved to know nothing while I was with you except Jesus Christ and him crucified. I came to you in weakness and fear, and with much trembling. My message and my preaching were not with wise and persuasive words, but with a demonstration of the Spirit's power, so that your faith might not rest on men's wisdom, but on God's power." —1 CORINTHIANS 2:1–5

These lessons appeal to a diverse group, including people who have never heard the gospel, as well as people who might be regular students of the Word, but have somehow missed how it all points to the big picture of salvation. We include insights about how each lesson/story connects to God's purpose, but we avoid areas that might confuse. For the person wrestling with the gospel (which, we pray, is the case), too much detail could distract from the simple gospel truth: *Jesus saves.* We avoid too much detail as well as lessons that could have different interpretations. Simply, these lessons focus on main Bible truths that reveal God unfolding His plan of salvation.

You choose how to use these lessons with your group.

Your lesson time. Please note that there is plenty of material for you to cover with students. However, you can customize lesson time length and what you will be able to cover in your group's schedule.

Your Bible version. Stepping Stones lessons use Scripture quoted from the Holy Bible, New International Version (1984). That's the version we've used successfully to teach these lessons in our classes. Whichever version you choose, you will see that the lesson truths remain the same, including what you'll find in the handout keys for teachers. Whatever Bible version you may choose, you can easily review and adapt your handout keys to that version.

Your handout keys. These are references that make lessons easy to teach. You can use the keys to help emphasize lesson content with your group.

Your student participant handouts and tools. There are helpful handouts for participants to refer to, such as the books of the Bible, and so on. There are dramatic play scripts. In addition, there are handouts that review lesson facts and principles, just like your teacher handout keys—but without the answers. If you would like to use these tools with your group, you can easily locate the *Stepping Stones* Student Handouts at NewHopePublishers.com, the site for the trade publishing division of WMU®.

11

Your lesson application activities. You'll also find lessons include suggestions for students to apply to life what the lessons teach. There are other creative activities, including visuals you may choose to use, group work, pair work, plays, discussions, movies, and more that will help carry students forward through God's unfolding plan of salvation. Feel free to customize these to best fit your group.

Your steps. Stepping Stones outlines each lesson, step by step from overview to conclusion, providing tried-and-true ways to use *Stepping Stones* successfully.

We pray these lessons will be a blessing to you and your participants as *Stepping Stones* has allowed us to share God's unfolding plan of salvation with many. We invite you to share your testimonies at: NewHopeReader@wmu.org

—Rita, Melanie, Amanda

More About Customizing the Content for Your Group

What's included and how to teach it

There are 26 lessons in this Bible study. Some are more foundational than others. Four of the lessons are "Optional Lessons" because, while they are wonderful stories that teach important truths, they do not directly answer the question, "What does a person need to know to be saved?" That said, you may find these optional lessons helpful with your participants. Some are fun to teach. Two of them are dramas (Jonah and John 9) that your class can act out together. If you do include any optional lessons in your schedule, you will want to teach in the chronological order of the other lessons you teach. For example, the optional lesson on John 9 can substitute for Lesson 13, Jesus, Miracles. The last two optional lessons are on the Cross and Resurrection and use the film, *The Passion of the Christ*.

Each *Stepping Stone* lesson provides teachers with advance preparation and outlined teaching notes about each step of the lesson, including:

- Materials needed
- Overview of lesson objective(s)
- Teaching steps
- Review steps
- Application-to-life steps
- Next steps, and more

Time and key points of the lessons

Each of these lessons takes about one hour to teach. You can use the entire lesson, or choose key points. The teacher should study these lessons and Bible passages carefully in advance, deciding what to include from the lesson for the group engaged in learning, in order to communicate successfully these items:

> - **Key Figure**
> - **Key Word**
> - **Key Concept**
> - **Key Scripture**

This will be especially important if the class meets for less than one hour.

Whether you and your participants meet for an hour, less than an hour, or more than an hour, it will be important to review the lesson outline in advance, making it your own, and determining how to manage the prayertimes, participant handouts, and teacher-handout keys with **answers underlined and**

in bold print within each lesson's notes. You may want to highlight throughout the lesson those key Scripture verses you will plan to focus on; see in advance the Scripture reference verses throughout the lesson outlines. Simply highlight, circle, or place a check ✓ at the key Scriptures and supporting Scriptures you will study, and then emphasize during lessons.

Your options for customizing the study for a shorter session

If you do not have 20 class meetings in your session, please consider the following when determining what to include in the class schedule.

1. This Bible study shows how the Bible is one story of the redemption of mankind. The schedule should include lessons on how human life began, what went wrong, how God addressed the problem, how God kept His promises, and what that means for us.

2. Choose and teach lessons in the order in which they are presented in this study. This is how students will begin to get a feel for God's progressive revelation and for His faithfulness to His purposes.

3. The schedule should include the lessons on the Cross and the Resurrection and the gospel presentation. Without these lessons, the whole point is lost, namely, that Jesus died for mankind's sin and that each person must receive God's gracious gift by faith (Ephesians 2:8–9).

4. Here is a suggested, abbreviated schedule of lessons:
   - Creation: how it all began and why
   - The Fall: what went wrong
   - Abraham, Part 2: the sacrifice of Isaac, mentioning how Jesus fulfilled it
   - Joseph, Part 1 and 2: forgiveness and living righteously even when it is hard
   - Moses, Part 1: his life story with some mention about Passover to prepare them for Jesus who fulfills it
   - David, Part 2: David and Bathsheba, receiving forgiveness—even of terrible sins
   - Jesus: as many lessons as you have time for; preparing them for the gospel, and including the Cross and Resurrection
   - The Gospel: use a systematic presentation with which you are comfortable; call for personal response. (Lesson 16, Why the Cross? calls for a response at the end of the lesson and can be used instead of Lesson 18: The Good News.)

- Peter and Paul if you have time: how life changes after response to the gospel

5. You can also teach this study successfully in 12 class meetings using this abbreviated schedule:
   - Class 1   Creation, the Fall
   - Class 2   Abraham
   - Class 3   Joseph
   - Class 4   Moses
   - Class 5   David
   - Class 6   Jesus' Prophecies and Birth
   - Class 7   Jesus' Miracles (or the optional Lesson on John 9)
   - Class 8   Jesus' Teachings
   - Class 9   The Cross
   - Class 10   The Resurrection
   - Class 11   Why the Cross? (gospel presentation)
   - Class 12   How the Gospel Changes a Life: Peter and Paul

Prayer

You'll find preparation tips for lessons, suggestions for introductions, and materials needed listed at the start of each Bible study lesson. Most importantly, begin this study and each lesson with prayer! We pray with you that many lives will be touched with the gospel and many will come to understand the salvation God has promised all Christian believers.

 Creation

Stepping Stones

> - Key Figure: God
> - Key Word: Create
> - Key Concept: God created us for relationship.
> - Key Scriptures: Genesis 1–2

Materials Needed: Find lesson handouts for participants, available online. If you know the name of each participant, have an index card ready for each of them, with name, meaning of participant's name, and a Scripture verse.

OVERVIEW
Lesson Objectives
- Overview of the Bible
- I am created by God and in His image.
- I am special to God.
- God has purposes for me.
- God knows my name.

Step 1   Class Introductions
- Pray—be sure to begin every lesson with prayer.
- Class Introductions
- Discuss Course Schedule
  - What we will be doing in this Bible study course
    - Chronological study of the Bible
    - Beginning with Creation, through the Old Testament, up to the Cross
    - "Jumping mountaintops": hitting highlights, not every story
  - Note the schedule and Bible characters to be studied. See Table of Contents.

Step 2   Origin and Organization of the Bible; Translations
- Point to "The Bible Is Unique" handout.
  - Read over pages 21–23. Note the origin of the Bible.
  - Look at pages 21–23. Note the organization of the Bible.
    - Note the different sections (that is, historical, poetry, and so on).

15

- Note that the Bible as it is generally packaged is not in actual chronological order.
- Search the *Stepping Stones* handouts at NewHopePublishers.com for short summaries of each book.
- We will be referring to this handout throughout the study to see where the stories we study fit into the overall picture.
- Discuss Translations
  - Original Languages: see "The Bible Is Unique" handout, page 22.
  - Translations
    - Ask, "Do any of you read Hebrew or Greek?" Allow answers. Explain, "That is why we need a translation into our language, English, Spanish, or other."
    - The Bible has also been translated into Italian, French, Chinese, Arabic, Korean, and more.
    - Sometimes language in a country changes over time. Words change in meaning. This also creates a need for a new translation.
  - Encourage participants to choose a translation for their regular study.
    - Some are more literal.
    - Some use older language.
    - Most are good; choosing one you are comfortable with is key.
    - Avoid a paraphrase for Bible study.
  - It is sometimes helpful to compare verses in several versions or translations.
    - This can bring more light to a verse and passage.

★ **Ask**

"Are you ready to begin our study of the Bible?"

Step 3   Introduce Genesis
- Meaning of the word *Genesis*: origins, beginnings
- What God begins here in Genesis, He completes in the rest of the Bible and human history.

Step 4   God Creates
- Genesis 1:1: In the beginning, *God*
  - God was all there was, but what a great start!
  - God is the main character.
  - He created the heavens and the earth.
- Read aloud or skim Genesis 1–2:3. Have participants note the significance of the days of creation by circling first, second, third, and so on in their Bible with a pencil, and have them note what is created each day on their handouts.

GENESIS 1 — GOD CREATES

VERSES	DAY	WHAT WAS CREATED
3–5	Day 1	**Light**; **Day and Night**
		saw that the light was **good** (v. 4)
6–8	Day 2	**Sky** (heavens)
9–13	Day 3	**Dry land, Seas, Plants** (according to their various kinds)
		saw that it was **good** (vv. 10, 12)
14–19	Day 4	**Sun, Moon, Stars** (to separate day from night and signs to mark seasons)
		saw that it was **good** (v. 18)
20–23	Day 5	**Sea creatures** (v. 21), **Birds** (according to their kind) saw that it was **good** (vv. 24–31)
	Day 6	**Land animals, Reptiles** (according to their kinds)
		saw that it was **good** (v. 25)
		Mankind (like us, for a purpose); it was **very good** (v. 31)
		Note the different wording here
		after everything was complete, it was **very** good.

Week 1
Lesson 1
17

- What words does God use to describe the creative process? *said, created, made*
  - Notice that before God created, there was nothing. Genesis 1:1
  - Hebrews 11:3 tells us, "By faith we understand that the universe was formed at God's command, so that what is seen was not made out of what was visible."
    - God created by His command, that is, by speaking.
    - He did not create by using something that already existed.
  - When man creates, he must begin with materials that God has made.
  - Only God can create something out of nothing.
- What is God's assessment of His creation? good, very good

Step 5 God Creates Man and Woman
- God's creation of man and woman was special and unique. Note the differences in the creation of mankind compared to the creation of the animals.
  - Does not say **"Let there be man."** God says, **"Let us make man."** Genesis 1:26
    - "make" is more personal than "let there be"

- **"In his own image, in the image of God."** Genesis 1:27
  - God is making mankind in His own image.
  - Humans are unique. They are not animals.
- Genesis 2:7, 21–22 details the creation of man and woman and shows it to be a very personal creative act. (Genesis 2 is not chronological, but it gives us a more detailed account of the creation of mankind.)
  - Note the words used—*formed, breathed*, Genesis 2:7; *made,* Genesis 2:22
    - ○ God breathes into man the breath of life. Genesis 2:7
    - ○ This is both physical and spiritual life.
    - ○ This is not done to the animals.
  - God created woman for mankind's well-being. Genesis 2:18
  - A very hands-on action. Genesis 2:21–22
    - ○ Psalm 139:13–15 uses the words *knit* and *weave*.
- God created man and woman with purposes in mind.
  - Genesis 1:26–29 contains more detail about the purposes for which mankind was created.

  - **"Let them rule."** Genesis 1:26
  - **"Be fruitful and increase** . . . **fill the earth and subdue it** . . . Rule over . . . every living creature." Genesis 1:28
  - Genesis 2:5 says there is no man to **work the ground**.
    - This points to mankind's purpose.
    - The rest of creation was prepared for humanity, the crown of God's creation.
  - Genesis 2:15 Again, mankind's purpose
    - God put humans into the garden to **"work it and take care of it."**
    - Work is not a **curse**.
    - The ground was cursed, making the work difficult. Genesis 3:17–19
  - **Man names the animals.** Genesis 2:19–20
    This is related to "let them rule." Genesis 1:26

Step 6 Two Trees, One Law

- God planted two special trees in the middle of the garden. What are they? Genesis 2:9
  - **Tree of Life**
  - **Tree of the Knowledge of Good and Evil**
- He only gave man one restriction or law. What was it? Genesis 2:16–17
  - **He was free to eat from any tree in the garden except the Tree of the Knowledge of Good and Evil.**
- What was the consequence of violating the law?
  - **You will die.**

Step 7　God Finished Creating

- "The man and his wife were both naked, and they felt no shame." Genesis 2:25 This was to be the normal state of the man and woman.
- What did God do after He finished creating? Genesis 2:1–3
  - He **finished** the work He had been doing.
  - He **rested**.
  - He **blessed** the seventh day and made it **holy**.

Step 8　Summary

- Who created the world? God
- Was it an accident? No, He had purposes in mind.
- What was the crown of His creation? Man (that's us!)
  - Said His creation of man was very good
  - Previous creation was preparation for man
- Why did God create?
  - For relationship
  - This is not as obvious from chapters 1 and 2. See Genesis 3:8–9: God is walking in the garden in the cool of the day looking for them so He can have fellowship with them.

- Other Bible verses point to the relationship God wants to have with mankind.
  - **God tells Moses, "I have known you by name."** Exodus 33:12–17
  - Look at Isaiah 43:1, 7.
    - **These verses use the words: *formed, created, made* (Genesis words).**
    - **God says to Israel, "I have called you by name . . . you were created for My glory."**
  - **God tells Jeremiah that He knew him even before He formed him in the womb.** Jeremiah 1:5
  - **Jesus tells us that our hairs are numbered and we are more valuable than sparrows.** Matthew 10:29–31

★ Application to Life

What does this mean for us?
- God knows my name and wants a relationship with me.
- If possible, pass out an index card to each student with their name, meaning of their name, and a Scripture verse.

Step 9　Next Steps

- In the next lesson, we will discuss what went wrong — sin, the Fall — but here we see why the Fall was so serious.

- If we were not valuable, then not much was lost.
- But God will spend the rest of the Bible (and human history) working to recover what was lost: His relationship with us.
- Later in this course we will see that He will even sacrifice His only Son, Jesus, to make that relationship possible.
- Give the students some suggestions for starting a daily quiet time.
  - Read a little each day.
  - Reflect and ask God to teach you.
  - Note that Bible study works like other things in life; you get out of it in proportion to what you put into it.
- Pray.

★ Note to Teacher

We once got the following question when we were talking about the two trees in the Garden of Eden: "If God knows everything and knew we would fail, why did He create the Tree of the Knowledge of Good and Evil?"

SOME THOUGHTS ON THIS:

1. God created man with a free will. His intention was for mankind to be good and to live forever, but He gave them a choice and mankind chose. Some believe that real love cannot be forced. Mankind could not truly love God if there were no other choice.

2. God did not create sin or evil. James 1:13–15 says that God does not tempt anyone; instead they are dragged away by their evil desires giving birth to sin and death.

3. Sometimes God tests people to reveal what is in them: Are they humble? Is their love or faith genuine? His goal may be to be reconciled to them or to refine their character.

ORIGIN AND ORGANIZATION OF THE BIBLE

The Bible is unique—one of a kind
The Best of Josh McDowell: A Ready Defense, describes the Holy Bible:

Here is a book . . .
- Written over a 1,500-year span
- Written over 40 generations

Written by more than 40 authors:
From every walk of life, including kings, peasants, philosophers, fishermen, poets, statesmen, scholars, and so on.
- Moses, a political leader, trained in the universities of Egypt
- Peter, a fisherman
- Amos, a herdsman
- Joshua, a military general
- Nehemiah, a cupbearer
- Daniel, a prime minister
- Luke, a doctor
- Solomon, a king
- Matthew, a tax collector
- Paul, a rabbi

Written in different places:
- Moses in the wilderness
- Jeremiah in a dungeon
- Daniel on a hillside and in a palace
- Paul inside prison walls
- Luke while traveling
- John on the isle of Patmos
- Others in the rigors of a military campaign

Written at different times:
- David in times of war
- Solomon in times of peace

Written during different moods:
- Some writing from the heights of joy
- Others from the depth of sorrow and despair

Written on three continents:
- Asia, Africa, Europe

Written in three languages:

- Hebrew — In 2 Kings 18:26–28 called "the language of Judah"; in Isaiah 19:18 called "the language of Canaan"
- Aramaic — the common language of the Near East until the time of Alexander the Great (from the 6th century BC to the 4th century BC)
- Greek — the New Testament language (The international language at the time of Christ)

Finally, its subject matter includes hundreds of controversial topics. Yet, the biblical authors spoke with harmony and continuity from Genesis to Revelation. There is one unfolding story: "God's redemption of man."

THE 39 OLD TESTAMENT BOOKS

17 Historical	5 Poetical	17 Prophetic
Genesis	Job	Isaiah
Exodus	Psalm	Jeremiah
Leviticus	Proverbs	Lamentations
Numbers	Ecclesiastes	Ezekiel
Deuteronomy	Song of Songs	Daniel
Joshua		Hosea
Judges		Joel
Ruth		Amos
1 Samuel		Obadiah
2 Samuel		Jonah
1 Kings		Micah
2 Kings		Nahum
1 Chronicles		Habakkuk
2 Chronicles		Zephaniah
Ezra		Haggai
Nehemiah		Zechariah
Esther		Malachi

THE 27 NEW TESTAMENT BOOKS

4 Gospels	Acts	21 Epistles		Revelation
Matthew	Acts	Romans	Titus	Revelation
Mark		1 Corinthians	Philemon	
Luke		2 Corinthians	Hebrews	
John		Galatians	James	
		Ephesians	1 Peter	
		Philippians	2 Peter	
		Colossians	1 John	
		1 Thessalonians	2 John	
		2 Thessalonians	3 John	
		1 Timothy	Jude	
		2 Timothy		

Halley's Bible Handbook describes the Bible book divisions in this way:

Historical:	Rise and Fall of the Hebrew Nation.
Poetical:	Literature of the Nation's (Israel's) Golden Age.
Prophetic:	Literature of the Nation's (Israel's) Dark Days.
Gospels:	The MAN (JESUS) whom the Nation Produced.
Acts:	His Reign among All Nations Begins.
Epistles:	His Teachings and Principles.
Revelation:	Forecast of His Universal Dominion.

Halley also shares how some of the Bible books have a principal thought, while other Bible books are about a number of things. This information is available online.

What did God create on each day? What did He think about His creation?

Day 1 (Genesis 1:3–5)
He created
Light (darkness already existing), separated them; called the light "day" and gave darkness the name "night."
- Saw that the light was **good**. Genesis 1:4

Day 2 (Genesis 1:6–8)
He created
The "sky" (the expanse to separate water above from water below vv. 7–8).

Day 3 (Genesis 1:9–13)
He created
Seas and land, vegetation.
- Saw that it was **good**. Genesis 1:10, 12

Day 4 (Genesis 1:14–19)
He created
Stars, sun, moon; to separate day from night and to serve as signs to mark seasons and days and years.
- Saw that it was **good**. Genesis 1:18

Day 5 (Genesis 1:20–23)
He created
Sea creatures, birds. (v. 22 God blessed them; be fruitful and increase.)
- Saw that it was **good**. Genesis 1:21

Day 6 (Genesis 1:24–31)
He created
Livestock, land animals, wild animals (vv. 24–25)
- Saw that it was **good**. Genesis 1:25
Man—in our image (v. 26); they would rule over the earth and the creatures (v. 26); male and female (v. 27).
- Saw all that He had made, and it was **very good**. Genesis 1:31

God's creation of man and woman was special and unique.
- God does not say, "**Let there be man.**"
- He does say:
  - Genesis 1:26 "**Let us make man in our image, in our likeness.**"
  - Genesis 1:27 "**in his own image, in the image of God**"

His creation of mankind is a *very personal* act. Note the words He used in these verses:

- Genesis 2:7 "**formed** from dust, **breathed** into his nostrils life"
- Genesis 2:21–22 "**made** a woman"

God has purposes for mankind.
- Genesis 1:26 **let them rule** *over all the earth*
- Genesis 1:28 **be fruitful and increase in number; fill the earth and subdue it**
- Genesis 2:5 **work the ground**
- Genesis 2:15 **work (the land) and take care of it**
  - Work is not a **curse**. Work is part of our purpose.
- Genesis 2:19–20 **Man names the animals.**

Two Trees, One Law

God planted two special trees in the middle of the garden. What are they?
Genesis 2:9

- **The Tree of Life and the Tree of the Knowledge of Good and Evil**

God gave man one restriction or law. What was it? What was the consequence?
Genesis 2:16–17

- **Not to eat from the Tree of the Knowledge of Good and Evil; you will surely die.**

What did God do when He finished creating? Genesis 2:1–3
- He **finished** the work He had been doing.
- He **rested**.
- He **blessed** the seventh day and made it **holy**.

Other Bible verses that point to the relationship God wants to have with mankind:
- Exodus 33:12–17 **God tells Moses, "I have known you by name."**
- Isaiah 43:1, 7 **These verses use the words** *formed, created, made.* **These are Genesis words. God tells Isaiah, "I have called you by name . . . you were created for My glory."**
- Jeremiah 1:5 **God tells Jeremiah that He knew him even before He formed him in the womb.**
- Matthew 10:29–31 **Jesus tells us that our hairs are numbered and we are more valuable than sparrows.**

The Fall of Man

Stepping Stones

> ➤ Key Figures: Adam and Eve
> ➤ Key Words: Sin and Disobedience
> ➤ Key Concept: Sin separates us from God, but God provides a remedy.
> ➤ Key Scripture: Genesis 3

Materials Needed: Find lesson handouts for participants, available online. Bring an apple for a visual aid when Adam and Eve eat the fruit. (optional)

OVERVIEW

Lesson Objectives

- God created a perfect world.
- God created mankind to live in His perfect world and to have relationship with Him, but something went wrong.
- God had given mankind the ability to choose.
- Man disobeyed God and the world was changed forever.
- God did not abandon mankind. He took immediate steps to protect him and made the first promise of a Savior.

Step 1   Begin the Lesson

- Pray—be sure to begin every lesson with prayer.
- Today we will see that even though God created a perfect world and placed mankind in a lovely garden, something went wrong that changed the world forever.

Step 2   Review Last Lesson

- Ask students to recount what they learned in the last lesson.
- In our last lesson we saw that God had created a perfect world and placed mankind in it.
- He had created mankind for relationship with Him.
- We saw that there were two trees in the Garden of Eden where God had placed mankind, the Tree of Life and the Tree of the Knowledge of Good and Evil. Genesis 2:9

- God gave mankind only one restriction and a consequence. He was allowed to eat from any tree in the garden except the Tree of the Knowledge of Good and Evil. If they ate from it they would die. Genesis 2:16–17

Step 3 Present the Whole Story—Genesis 3:1–24
- Retell or read the whole passage with feeling.
- Bring an apple—simply as a prop as apples weren't native to the region—and show it when the tree is mentioned. Take a bite of it when Eve eats the fruit in the story.

Step 4 Who Was the Serpent?—Genesis 3:1
- Establish the craftiness of the serpent.
  - Look at Genesis 3:1. How is the serpent described?
    - The serpent is described as **crafty** in the Bible.
    - What does "crafty" mean?
      - Suggestions: **deceitful, sneaky, sly, cunning, wily, tricky, scheming**
- How does the serpent first entice Eve to desire the fruit?
  - He asks her a question, "**Did God really say**?"
  - He is questioning God's authority and planting seeds of doubt in her mind.

Step 5 Eve Misquotes God—Genesis 3:2–3
- Have someone read Genesis 3:2–3 aloud.
- What did God originally command about the Tree of the Knowledge of Good and Evil? Look back at Genesis 2:16–17.
  - **He told them not to eat from that tree or they would surely die.**
- Was Eve's statement about God's original command correct? **No**
- What was different about her interpretation? **She added to the command when she said they weren't to touch it**.

Step 6 The Temptation of Sin—Genesis 3:4–6
- Have someone read Genesis 3:4–6 aloud. Now the temptation continues in earnest.
- First the serpent directly contradicts God when he says that she will not die. Genesis 2:17; 3:4
- Then he plants doubt about the goodness of God and implies that God is holding out on them, keeping them from something they would want. Genesis 3:5
- What does Eve notice about the fruit when she looks at it? Genesis 3:6
  - It is **good** for **food**.
  - It is **pleasing** to the **eye**.
  - It is **desirable** for **gaining wisdom**.

- Read 1 John 2:16.
  - Notice the things that John mentions that are not from the Father but from the world.
    - the **lust** of the **flesh**
    - the **lust** of the **eyes**
    - the **pride** of **life**
  - How are these similar to what Eve sees in the fruit?
    - The serpent (Satan) is still using the same three tactics on us that worked on Eve.
    - The things that tempt us fall into these three categories:
      - ○ **What makes us feel good and comfortable**
      - ○ **Things we see**
      - ○ **Pride**
- Adam and Eve sin. Genesis 3:6
  - After Eve is tempted, she eats some of the fruit and gives some to her husband who was with her, and he eats it too.

Step 7   **The Consequences of Sin—Genesis 3:7–8, 10**

- Look at Genesis 3:7–8, 10. What happened immediately after Adam and Eve disobeyed God?
  - Their eyes were **opened**.
  - They realized that they were **naked**.
  - Then they attempted to **hide** from God.
  - They were **afraid**.
- Note that they did not die—physically—at least not yet. But their behavior shows that the spiritual relationship they had with God is dead. Also, death entered the world, and someday they would die physically as well.

Step 8   **Adam and Eve's Response—Genesis 3:9–13**

- Read Genesis 3:9–13.
- When God calls to him asking where he is, Adam explains that he is naked and afraid, so he is hiding.
  - Why do you think Adam and Eve attempt to hide from God?
- What is Adam's excuse when God confronts him about his sin? Genesis 3:12
  - Adam actually appears to blame **God**, as well as the woman: "The woman You put here gave me fruit and I ate it."
- What is Eve's excuse when God speaks to her about her sin? Genesis 3:13
  - Eve blames the **serpent**: "The serpent deceived me and I ate."
- Notice that both of them blame someone else rather than take responsibility for their sin.

- Although Adam and Eve gave excuses, God held them both accountable and did not dismiss their sin.

Step 9   God's Response to Their Sin—Genesis 3:8–9, 14–19

- Look again at Genesis 3:8–9. How does God show that He wants relationship with them?
  - God is walking in the garden looking for them.
  - God created man for relationship.
  - It appears that He came regularly to fellowship with them.
- After He confronts the man and the woman about their sin, He punishes all parties involved in the sin, beginning with the serpent.
  - God curses the serpent. Genesis 3:14–15:
    - **To be lowlier than the beasts of the earth**
    - **To have enmity with woman**
  - God punishes the woman. Genesis 3:16:
    - **To have increased pain in childbirth**
    - **To have a desire for her husband, and he shall rule over her**
  - God curses the ground: thus increasing the difficulty of man's work. Remember that work is not a curse, but now:

    - **The ground is cursed and will produce thorns and thistles.**
    - **Man will have to work in painful toil and by the sweat of his brow.**
    - **He will work hard all his life until he returns to the ground, a reference to physical death.**
- Where is the bright spot in all this? God shows mercy and grace and provides a remedy.
  - God gives the first promise of a Savior. Look at Genesis 3:15.
    - **God puts enmity between the serpent and offspring (seed) of the woman.**
    - Notice also that **the "seed" will crush the serpent's head** (a life-ending blow), but the serpent will strike the heel of the "seed" (only a wound).
    - This is the first promise of a Savior and is a reference to Jesus Christ.
      - On the Cross, the serpent wounded Jesus, who died and rose again, but Jesus dealt Satan a crushing blow and won the victory. Have someone read 1 Corinthians 15:54–57.
  - God gives them proper covering. Genesis 3:21
    - The only acceptable sacrifice for sin is a blood sacrifice. Have someone read Hebrews 9:22.
    - Adam and Eve made for themselves coverings of plants. Genesis 3:7
    - **God sacrifices an animal and makes coverings of skin for them.**
    - **This is the first death in the perfect world God has made.**
    - Adam and Eve now begin to see what their sin will cost.

- God protects them from living forever in sin. Genesis 3:22–24
  - Remember the other tree in the garden? The Tree of Life.
  - God banishes the couple from the garden and places an angel with a flaming sword to guard the Tree of Life.
  - <u>He is protecting them from eating from this Tree and living forever in their sin. They need to have their sin paid for before they live forever.</u>

Step 10 Next Steps
- Now we know why the world is not perfect the way it was after the creation.
- Adam and Eve disobeyed God and brought sin and death into the world.
- God punished their sin, but He also protected them and promised a remedy.
- As we go through the Bible, we will see how God keeps that promise.

HANDOUT KEY: LESSON 2—THE FALL OF MAN

Who Was the Serpent?—Genesis 3:1
- The serpent is described as <u>crafty</u> in the Bible.
- This word can mean <u>deceitful, sneaky, sly, cunning, wily, tricky, scheming</u>.
- The serpent begins by asking Eve the question: <u>"Did God really say?"</u>

Eve Misquotes God—Genesis 3:2–3
What did God originally command about the Tree of the Knowledge of Good and Evil? Genesis 2:16–17
- <u>He told them not to eat from that tree or they would surely die.</u>

Was Eve's statement about God's original command correct? <u>No</u>
What was different about her interpretation?
- <u>She added to the command when she said they weren't to touch it.</u>

The Temptation of Sin—Genesis 3:4–6
What does Eve notice about the fruit when she looks at it? Genesis 3:6. It was:
- <u>good</u> for <u>food</u>
- <u>pleasing</u> to the <u>eye</u>
- <u>desirable</u> for <u>gaining wisdom</u>

Notice the things John mentions in 1 John 2:16 that are not from the Father but from the world:
- <u>lust</u> of the <u>flesh</u>
- <u>lust</u> of the <u>eyes</u>
- <u>pride</u> of <u>life</u>

What do these things represent?
- <u>What makes us feel good and comfortable</u>

- Things we see
- Pride

The Consequences of Sin—Genesis 3:7–8, 10
What were the immediate consequences of Adam and Eve's sin?
- Their eyes were **opened**.
- They realized that they were **naked**.
- Then they attempted to **hide** from God.
- They were **afraid**.

Adam and Eve's Response—Genesis 3:9–13
Why do you think Adam and Eve attempt to hide from God?

Adam appears to blame **God**, as well as the woman.
Eve blames the **serpent**.

God's Response to Their Sin—Genesis 3:8–9, 14–19
God cursed the serpent:
- **To be lowlier than the beasts of the earth; to have enmity with the woman**
God punished the woman:
- **To have increased pain in childbirth**
- **To have a desire for her husband, and he shall rule over her**
God cursed the ground:
- **To grow food, man will have to work hard all his life until he returns to the ground (physical death)**

Week 1
Lesson 2
31

God Shows Mercy and Grace and Provides a Remedy
The first promise of a Savior—Genesis 3:15
- **He puts enmity between the serpent and her offspring and promises that the offspring will crush the head of the serpent (a death blow).**
Proper covering—Genesis 3:21
- **God sacrifices an animal and makes coverings of skin for them.**
Protection—Genesis 3:22–24
- **He protects them from eating from the Tree of Life and living forever in their sin before their sin is paid for.**

Abraham's Story, Part 1— God Chooses a Family

Stepping Stones

> ➤ Key Figure: Abraham
> ➤ Key Word: Faith
> ➤ Key Concept: God chooses a family to bless the world.
> ➤ Key Scriptures: Genesis 12; 15–18; 21

Preparation: (Optional) Write the notes and Scripture references from Step 3 on the board. Students may want to write down this information, but you will not have enough time to explain each verse during the lesson. Use this as an introductory overview of man's lineage and history prior to God's encounter with Abraham. Find lesson handouts for participants, available online.

OVERVIEW

Lesson Objectives

- Man continued to fall into greater evil after the Fall.
- God chooses a family to bless the world.
- God speaks and Abraham responds in faith.

Step 1   Begin the Lesson

- Pray—be sure to begin every lesson with prayer.
- Today we will begin Abraham's story by looking at several times that God spoke to Abraham and how Abraham responded.

Step 2   Review Last Lesson

- In our last lesson we reviewed what went wrong after God created a perfect world.
- We saw that Adam and Eve, the first man and woman, listened to the serpent and disobeyed God.
- God responded by cursing the serpent, punishing the couple, and cursing the ground.

Step 3 **Period Since the Fall**

- After the Fall, man becomes progressively worse. Briefly present the following information to show this.
  - Genesis 4—Adam and Eve's first son, Cain, kills their second son, Abel, in a fit of jealousy.
  - Genesis 5:4—Adam and Eve have other children.
    - Genesis 5 traces the genealogy from Adam to Noah.
  - Genesis 6:5–8—After a period of time following Adam, "The LORD saw how great man's wickedness on earth had become, and that every inclination of the thoughts of his heart was only evil all the time." God is grieved and decides to wipe mankind from the face of the earth by flood. One man, Noah, and his family are saved.
  - Genesis 9:1—Mankind starts over and is once again commanded to "be fruitful and increase in number and fill the earth."
  - Genesis 10 traces the genealogy of Noah.
  - Genesis 11—Mankind becomes corrupt again and conspires against God and His ways at the Tower of Babel. God confuses their language and scatters them over the whole earth in order to slow them down.
    - Genesis 11:10–26 traces the genealogy from Noah to Abram.
  - At the end of Genesis 11:
    - Genesis 11:30—Abram's wife is barren.
    - Notice the name—Abram. Later God will change his name to Abraham.
    - Genesis 11:31—The family is living in Haran.
    - Genesis 11:32—Abram's father dies.
- Briefly discuss Abram's background and family overview. Genesis 11:24–27
  - Descendant of Noah
  - Terah, Abram's father, worships idols (see Joshua 24:2, 14).
  - Abram is just **an ordinary guy!**

DISCUSSION QUESTION

Why would God want to initiate an encounter with an ordinary person?

Reference Nehemiah 9:7–8: "You are the LORD God, who chose Abram and brought him out of Ur of the Chaldeans and named him Abraham. **You found his heart faithful to you,** and you made a covenant with him to give to his descendants the land of the Canaanites, Hittites, Amorites, Perizzites, Jebusites, and Girgashites. You have kept your promise because you are righteous."

Step 4   God Calls Abram—Genesis 12:1–9

- Read (or have someone read) Genesis 12:1–9.
- God speaks to Abram.
    - God initiates an encounter with Abram.
    - God requires a response of faith.
    - God is in complete control and has a plan.
    - What does God tell Abram to do? Genesis 12:1
        - Leave—his **country,** his **people,** his **father's household**—basically everything he knew, everything familiar.
        - Go to—the **land** I will **show you.**
        - Note, God does not tell him exactly where this land is, only that He will show Abram (Hebrews 11:8). So Abram will need to follow and be dependent on God to find it.

Genesis 12—Promises to Abram
What does God promise Abram? Genesis 12:2–3, 7 (Look for the "I will" statements that were made by God.) • I will make you a **great nation**. • I will **bless** you. • I will make your **name great**. • You will be a **blessing**. • I will **bless** those who **bless** you and **curse** those who **curse** you. • All the peoples on earth will be **blessed through you**. • I will give this **land** to your **offspring**.
Ask their opinion: Were God's blessings simply to give Abram stuff for himself?

Step 5   Abram's Response

- Review God's promises to Abram. What is the human perspective on these promises?
    - Descendants (offspring): Abram is **75 years old** (Genesis 12:4) and his wife is **barren**. Genesis 11:30
    - Land: Canaanites already **inhabit** it. Genesis 12:6
    - Great Nation: Abram is just an **ordinary guy** and he is **childless**!

★ Application to Life

Does our human perspective sometimes hinder our faith in God's promises? How so?

- Have them look at Genesis 12:4–9 again.
- What is Abram's response? Genesis 12:4 So Abram left as the Lord had told him.
  - Abram hears from God and responds **without knowing exactly where to go**. See also Hebrews 11:8.
  - Abram hears from the Lord and begins to move, no doubting!
  - Abram goes without complaining.
- Abram praises the Lord by doing what in Genesis 12:8? **Building an altar to the Lord**
- Notice the pattern: God **speaks**. Abram **responds**. This pattern will hold throughout the story of Abram.

Step 6   God Promises Abram a Son—Genesis 15
- Read Genesis 15:1. God speaks to Abram again.
  - What does He tell Abram?
    - Do not be **afraid**.
    - I am your **shield**, your very great **reward**.
  - Did you see that? What is Abram's reward? God Himself! Not descendants, land, or blessings, but God Himself. May it be so for us as well.
- Read Genesis 15:2–3. Abram is concerned. Why?
  - He is childless and another man will inherit his estate.
  - Reference Genesis 12:4. How old is Abram? **75**
    So Abram has a legitimate concern.

Genesis 15—Promises to Abram
Read Genesis 15:4–5. What does God say about Abram's concern?
This man will not be your heir. A son from your own body will be your heir. Your offspring will be as many as the stars in the heavens.

- Read Genesis 15:6. How does Abram respond? Abram believed God and it was credited to him as righteousness.
  - This is a **key verse in Scripture**.
  - How did Abram become righteous? **by faith**

DISCUSSION QUESTION
Why is our faith in the Lord considered righteous to Him? **See Hebrews 11:6 and Hebrews 11:8–12.**

> Hebrews 11:6 says that **"without faith it is impossible to please God**, because anyone who comes to him must believe that he exists and that he rewards those who earnestly seek him" (emphasis added).
>
> Hebrews 11:8–12 goes on to tell us that Abraham lived by faith in the promises God had made to him.

- In the New Testament, Paul will quote Genesis 15:6 in Romans 4:3 and in Galatians 3:6–9.
- Paul also begins his letter to the Romans telling us that righteousness is by faith from first to last. Romans 1:17
- Paul revisits this concept in Ephesians 2:8–10 and shows us the relationship of faith and works. We are saved by the grace of God through faith for good works.
- Salvation has always been by faith, not by works. It was so in Abraham's time and it is still so for us.

- Summarize Genesis 15:8–21. Abram asks how he will know.
  - God seals His promises with a covenant ceremony. See additional notes on covenant.
  - God also makes a prediction about a period of 400 years that his descendants will spend in Egypt. Genesis 15:13–16
    - This will not occur until after Abram has lived in peace and been buried at a good old age.
    - Abram's descendants will return to the land in the fourth generation.
    - We will see this prophecy come true in later lessons on Moses.

Step 7   Abram and His Wife Falter—Genesis 16

- Abram and Sarai, his wife, have been living in Canaan for 10 years. Genesis 16:3
- How old is Abram now? (Remember Genesis 12:4.) He is 85 years old.
- Sarai has gotten impatient for a child and hatches a plan for Abram to have a child by her maidservant, Hagar. Abram agrees and a son is born whom the angel of the Lord names Ishmael. Genesis 16:2–4
  - Culturally, this was not uncommon, so what Sarai is proposing is not unusual for their times. The neighbors would not have condemned them for this act.
  - However, it is not what God promised, and we see how this action poisons the relationship between Sarai and Hagar. It also causes problems for the Israelites in later generations, even up to our own times.
  - This is what happens when we try to help God out instead of walking in faith and waiting on His timing.

Step 8   The Covenant of Circumcision—Genesis 17

- Read Genesis 17:1–8.
- How old is Abram? <u>**99**</u> So how long has he been waiting for a son? <u>**24 years**</u>
  Genesis 17:1

DISCUSS THOROUGHLY: GENESIS 17:3–8, Promises to Abram

What <u>promises</u> does God make to Abram in this chapter?

- My covenant is with you.
- You will be the father of many of nations.
- No longer will you be called Abram (exalted father); your name will be Abraham (father of a multitude).
- I will make you very fruitful.
- I will make nations of you, and kings will come from you.
- I will establish my covenant as an everlasting covenant between me and you and your descendants . . . to be your God and the God of your descendants after you.
- I give the land of Canaan to you and your descendants as an everlasting possession.

Week 2
Lesson 3
37

DISCUSS THOROUGHLY: GENESIS 17:9–14, Requirements of the Covenant

Here for the first time, God spells out the <u>requirements of the Covenant</u>. What are they?

- <u>**You and your descendants must keep my Covenant.**</u>
- <u>**Every male, both family members and servants, who is eight days or older shall be circumcised.**</u>
- Any male not circumcised has broken the covenant and is cut off from his people.

- What is circumcision?
  - It represents a new relationship with God and identifies them with God's people.
  - It is not required for salvation. In Romans 4:9–13, Paul makes the case that Abraham was credited as righteous before he was circumcised.
  - Circumcision was the seal or sign of the righteousness which Abraham had before he was circumcised. Romans 4:11

- In Romans 2:29 true circumcision is "of the heart, by the Spirit, not by the written code." This is what the prophets repeatedly came after Israel about and what Jesus criticized the Pharisees for—religion that was external but not from the heart.
- For New Testament believers, baptism serves a similar purpose. We believe first, and then are baptized. Baptism symbolizes and seals what has happened in the heart.
- Read Genesis 17:15–22.
  - Here God changes the name of Abraham's wife Sarai to Sarah and makes the first specific promise of a son to her. Note that the promises to Sarah are the same as the ones God made to Abraham.

Genesis 17:15–16, 21—Promises to Sarah

- I will bless her.
- I will surely give Abraham a son by her.
- I will bless her so that she will be the mother of nations.
- Kings of peoples will come from her.
- Her son will be born in one year.

- Abraham laughs at the idea of a 90-year-old woman having a child and asks if Ishmael could have the blessing. Genesis 17:17–18
  - God makes promises for Ishmael, but clearly states that His covenant is with Isaac. Genesis 17:19–21
  - Note to teacher: Paul discusses the difference between Hagar and Ishmael and Sarah and Isaac in Galatians 4:21–31 when he discusses the difference between the Law (bondwoman) and Grace (free woman). (This is more scriptural support for salvation by grace, but it may be more than is necessary for the discussion in this lesson.)
- Read Genesis 17:23–24 (also verses 25–27 if time allows). How does Abraham respond? **He circumcises his whole household as directed by the Lord**.

Step 9 Isaac Is Born—Genesis 21

- Read Genesis 21:1–7. The happy day finally arrives. God begins fulfilling His great promises to Abraham and Sarah.
- Sarah conceives and bears a son in her old age.
  - How old is Abraham? **100** Genesis 21:5
  - How old is Sarah? **90** Genesis 17:17
- What does Isaac's name mean? **He laughs.** Genesis 21:6

- Why do you think they named him that?
  - **Because God told them to** Genesis 17:19
  - **Because they laughed at the idea that they could have children when they were so old** (Abraham in Genesis 17:17; Sarah in Genesis 18:12).
    - **And now they are laughing and want everyone to celebrate with them.** Genesis 21:6–7
- Abraham circumcises his son when he is eight days old in obedience to the covenant. Genesis 21:4

Step 10 Next Steps
- The Fall changed the relationship between God and man.
- God chose a family to work through in order to restore what was lost.
- Abraham shows us what a life of faith looks like.
- Abraham repeatedly hears God speak and responds to Him in obedience.
- God made wonderful promises to Abraham. Have the students look back over their notes of the promises made to Abraham. How many of them have come true up to this point in Abraham's story? Only a few.
- In the next lesson, God will test Abraham's faith.
- Pray.

ADDITIONAL NOTES ABOUT RIGHTEOUSNESS

What is righteousness?
Merriam-Webster's dictionary online gives the definition of *righteous* as:
1. acting in accord with divine or moral law: free from guilt or sin
2. morally right or justifiable [a righteous decision]

Can we achieve righteousness by ourselves?
- Isaiah 64:6: "All of us have become like one who is unclean, and all our righteous acts are like filthy rags; we all shrivel up like a leaf, and like the wind our sins sweep us away."

How then is righteousness attained?
- Romans 3:22: "This righteousness from God comes through faith in Jesus Christ to all who believe. There is no difference."
- Romans 4:5: "However, to the man who does not work but trusts God who justifies the wicked, his faith is credited as righteousness."
- Galatians 2:16: "Know that a man is not justified by observing the law, but by faith in Jesus Christ. So we, too, have put our faith in Christ Jesus that we may be justified by faith in Christ and not by observing the law, because by observing the law no one will be justified."

ADDITIONAL NOTES ABOUT COVENANTS

Definitions of covenant (noun)
Merriam-Webster's online dictionary gives the definition of *covenant* as:
1. a usually formal, solemn, and binding agreement
2. a written agreement or promise usually under seal between two or more parties especially for the performance of some action

OLD COVENANT (prior to Jesus' death and resurrection)
- Genesis 15:6: "Abram believed the Lord, and he credited it to him as righteousness."
- Deuteronomy 6:25: "And if we are careful to obey all this law before the Lord our God, as he has commanded us, that will be our righteousness."

NEW COVENANT (Jesus gave Himself up as the ultimate sacrifice for our sins.)
- 2 Corinthians 5:21: "God made him who had no sin to be sin for us, so that in him we might become the righteousness of God."

HANDOUT KEY: LESSON 3—ABRAHAM'S STORY, PART I—GOD CHOOSES A FAMILY

Abram is just **an ordinary guy**!
Why would God want to initiate an encounter with an ordinary person?
Nehemiah 9:7–8: **He found Abram's heart faithful.**

God Calls Abram — Genesis 12:1–9
What does God tell Abram to do? Genesis 12:1
- Leave — his **country**, his **people**, and his **father's household**.
- Go to — the **land** I will **show you**.

What does God promise Abram? Genesis 12:2–3, 7
- I will make you a **great nation;** I will **bless** you.
- I will make your **name great**.
- You will be a **blessing**.
- I will **bless** those who **bless** you and **curse** those who **curse** you.
- All the peoples on earth will be **blessed through you**.
- I will give this **land** to your **offspring**.

Abram's Response
What is the *human perspective* on these promises?
- Descendants: Abram is **75 years old** and his wife is **barren**.

- Land: Canaanites already **inhabit** it.
- Great Nation: Abram is just an **ordinary guy** and he is **childless**!

Does our human perspective sometimes hinder our faith in God's promises?
- Yet, Abram hears from God and responds **without knowing exactly where to go.** (Hebrews 11:8)
- Abram praises the Lord by doing what in Genesis 12:8? **Building an altar to the Lord**
- Notice the pattern: God **speaks**. Abram **responds**.

God Promises Abram a Son — Genesis 15
What does God tell Abram?
- Do not be **afraid**.
- I am your **shield,** your very great **reward**.
- Genesis 15:6 is a **key verse in Scripture**.
- How did Abram become righteous? **by faith**

Why is our faith in the Lord considered righteous to Him? See Hebrews 11:6 and Hebrews 11:8–12. (See also Romans 4:3, Galatians 3:6–9, Romans: 1:17, and Ephesians 2:8–10.)

The Covenant of Circumcision — Genesis 17
- How old is Abram? **99**
- How long has he been waiting for a son? **24 years**

What promises does God make to Abram in verses 3–8?
- **At least seven promises are listed in these verses.**

Here for the first time, God spells out the requirements of the covenant. What are they?
- **Descendants must keep the covenant.**
- **Every male in the household, eight days or older, must be circumcised.**

How does Abraham respond? Genesis 17:23–24
- **He circumcises his whole household as directed by the Lord.**

Isaac Is Born — Genesis 21
- When Isaac is born, how old is Abraham? **100** Genesis 21:5
- How old is Sarah? **90** Genesis 17:17
- What does Isaac's name mean? **He laughs.** Genesis 21:6
- Why do you think they named him that?
  - **Because God told them to** Genesis 17:19
  - **Because they laughed at the idea that they could have children when they were so old.**
  - **And now they are laughing and want everyone to celebrate with them.**

Abraham's Story, Part 2— God Tests Abraham's Faith

Materials Needed: Find lesson handouts for participants, available online. Provide hymnals or copies of the hymn "Standing on the Promises." (optional)

OVERVIEW
Lesson Objectives
- God has made wonderful promises to us.
- Can we trust Him no matter what?

Step 1 Begin the Lesson
- Pray—be sure to begin every lesson with prayer.
- Today we will see that when God tests Abraham's faith, Abraham passes the test and we'll see the reason he passes.

Step 2 Review Last Lesson
- In our last lesson we saw that man became progressively worse after the Fall.
- God chose a family to bless the world.
- We saw God speaking to Abraham and making promises to him, and we saw how each time Abraham responded in faith.
- The pattern is—God spoke; Abraham acted.

★ Application to Life

This pattern works the same for us
- God speaks.
- We obey.
- God works.
- We worship.

Step 3 Isaac, the Son of the Covenant
- How many children does Abraham have? Two: Ishmael and Isaac.
- How many of these children are included in the promises God made to Abraham? Only one: Isaac.

- In Genesis 17 when God changed Sarai's name to Sarah and promised a son by her, Abraham asked that Ishmael might live under God's blessing. Genesis 17:15–18
- God responded that he would bless Ishmael, but that He was establishing the covenant with the son, Isaac, who would be born to Sarah in one year. Genesis 17:19–21
- Abraham had waited a long time for this promised son: 25 years. (The first promise was when Abraham was 75. Genesis 12:4)
  - Finally the promised son was born. Abraham and Sarah named him Isaac, which means laughter.
  - Abraham was 100 years old and Sarah was 90 years old when Isaac was born.

Step 4 God Tests Abraham
- Read Genesis 22:1–2.
- How does God identify Isaac?
  - **Your son**
  - Your **only** son

  - Ishmael has been sent away. Genesis 21:8–21
  - Isaac is the only son given to Abraham in fulfillment of the promises and the covenant.
  - **Isaac**
  - Whom you **love**
  - Note: This same description could be applied to Jesus as well. .
- There is no question whom God is talking about.
- God is also very aware of what this son means to Abraham both in terms of the covenant (only son) and of Abraham's love for his son (whom you love).
- What is God asking Abraham to do?
  - He tells Abraham to sacrifice Isaac as a burnt offering.
  - On one of the mountains He will tell Abraham about.
  - This is similar to when He told Abraham to leave his family and go to a land He would show him (Genesis 12:1).

Step 5 Abraham Responds
- Read Genesis 22:3–10.
- Notice that Abraham once again responds immediately.
- This is the pattern of Abraham's life. God speaks; Abraham responds.
  - Notice also that they travel for three days before Abraham sees the place in the distance. Genesis 22:4
    - Imagine walking for three days knowing what you are about to do.

- It appears that Abraham is the only one who knows the full extent of what will take place.
- The others know there will be a sacrifice. They are not surprised about this because Abraham often builds altars and offers sacrifices to God.
- But no one knows exactly what God has asked Abraham to do.
- Even Isaac does not know what is coming. Genesis 22:7
- The first clue about Abraham's faith in this matter. Genesis 22:5
  - Notice that he tells the servants that "we" will worship and "we" will come back.
  - He knows that he is supposed to sacrifice Isaac, but he is equally sure that somehow Isaac is coming back with him.

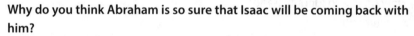

DISCUSSION QUESTIONS

Why do you think Abraham is so sure that Isaac will be coming back with him?
- <u>Isaac is the son of the promise</u>. If he does not come back somehow, then God can't be trusted to keep His promises.

Read Hebrews 11:17–19. The writer of Hebrews tells us why Abraham was able to do what God had asked him to do.
- He believed God's Word. He reasoned <u>that God could raise Isaac from the dead</u>.

Read Hebrews 6:13–20. We all have heard people say "I swear to God." Who does God swear by?
- Hebrews 6:13 says God swore <u>**by Himself**</u> when He made promises to Abraham because there is none greater for Him to swear by.
- Hebrews 6:17 says God confirmed His promises with an oath because He wanted to make very clear what was promised. After waiting patiently, Abraham received what was promised.

What does Hebrews 6:18 say is impossible?
- It is impossible <u>**for God to lie**</u>, so we may be greatly encouraged.

What does Hebrews 6:19 say about the hope this gives us?
- This hope is <u>**an anchor for our soul, firm and secure**</u>.

This is the key to faith and obedience. We need to remember that God has made promises to us. We can find out what these promises are in His Word, the Bible. If God did not keep His promises, then He would not be God. But He is God, and He is who He says He is, and He does what He says He will do. We can walk in hope, faith, and obedience because His promises are sure.

- Let us be faithful to God for the same reasons that Abraham was faithful.
- Genesis 15:6 "Abraham believed the Lord, and he credited it to him as righteousness."

- How old is Isaac? We are not really sure about this, but he is not a small child because Abraham places the wood on him for him to carry when they leave the servants to go and worship. Genesis 22:6
- While they are walking together, Isaac asks Abraham a question. "The fire and wood are here, but where is the lamb for the burnt offering?" Genesis 22:7
  - Here we see that Isaac does not know what God has asked Abraham to do.
  - Abraham does not answer Isaac directly. He only tells him that God Himself will provide the lamb. A statement of faith.
- They reach the place. Abraham binds Isaac and puts him on the altar and prepares to sacrifice him.
  - Note that Isaac appears to submit willingly. There is no mention of a struggle.

Step 6   Abraham Passes the Test
- Read Genesis 22:11–19.
- The Angel of the Lord calls to Abraham and stops him from sacrificing Isaac.
- What does the angel say that lets you know that Abraham has passed the test? **"Now I know that you fear God."**
- What reason does he give for Abraham passing the test?
  - He commends Abraham's **obedience.**
  - He repeats this three times.
    - Genesis 22:12 "because you have not withheld from me your son, your only son."
    - Genesis 22:16 "because you have done this and have not withheld your son, your only son."
    - Genesis 22:18 "because you have obeyed me."
- What promises does God repeat to Abraham now that he has passed the test? Genesis 22:17–18
  - **I will surely bless you.**
  - Descendants as **numerous** as **stars** and **sand**.
  - Descendants will **possess the cities of their enemies.**
  - **All the nations on earth** will be blessed through your offspring.

Step 7   The Substitution

- Notice Genesis 22:13–14 again.
- There was a sacrifice that day.
  - What was sacrificed? **A ram**
  - What did Abraham say that God would provide for the sacrifice? **A lamb** Genesis 22:8
- God did provide a sacrifice that day. It was a ram.
- Abraham called the place "The Lord Will Provide" in honor of His gift of the ram. Genesis 22:14
- Later God would provide other lambs for the sacrifice through the sacrificial system, which we will look at when we study Moses.
- One day God would provide the final Lamb He had promised. Read John 1:36. This is also the fulfillment of Genesis 3:15.

Step 8   Summary

- Hebrews 11:1 tells us that "faith is being sure of what we hope for and certain of what we do not see."

★ Application to Life

- Our hope is not like the world hopes, as in "I hope it doesn't rain."
- Our hope is in God who cannot lie and whose promises never fail. So it is a sure thing.
- When we are tested, we can pass the test by remembering God's character and His promises.

Step 9   Next Steps

- Sing "Standing on the Promises" together.
- In the next lesson, we will meet one of Abraham's descendants who knew how to stand on the promises of God.
- Pray.

HANDOUT KEY: LESSON 4—ABRAHAM'S STORY, PART 2—GOD TESTS ABRAHAM'S FAITH

God Tests Abraham

How does God identify Isaac? Genesis 22:2

- <u>Your son</u>
- Your <u>only</u> son

- Isaac
- Whom you **love**

Abraham Responds

Why do you think Abraham is so sure that Isaac will be coming back with him?

- **Isaac is the son of the promise.**
- He reasoned **that God could raise Isaac from the dead.** Hebrews 11:17–19
- Who does God swear by? **Himself** Hebrews 6:13
- It is impossible **for God to lie.** Hebrews 6:18
- This hope is **an anchor for our soul, firm and secure.** Hebrews 6:19

Abraham Passes the Test

What does the angel say that lets you know that Abraham has passed the test?

- Genesis 22:12: "**Now I know that you fear God.**"

What reason does he give for Abraham passing the test? (Repeated in Genesis 22:12, 16, 18)

- He commends Abraham's **obedience.**

What promises does God repeat to Abraham now that he has passed the test? Genesis 22:17–18

- **I will surely bless you.**
- Descendants as **numerous** as **stars** and **sand.**
- Descendants will **possess the cities of their enemies**.
- **All the nations on earth** will be blessed through your offspring.

The Substitution

What was sacrificed that day?

- Genesis 22:13–14 **A ram**

What did Abraham say that God would provide for the sacrifice?

- Genesis 22:8 **A lamb**

Joseph's Story, Part 1— Joseph in Potiphar's House

Stepping Stones
> Key Figure: Joseph
> Key Word: Trust
> Key Concept: God blesses us and others when we trust Him in trials.
> Key Scriptures: Genesis 37; 39

> **Focal Verse: Genesis 39:1–23**

> **Related Verses**
  * Ephesians 6:5–9
  * Colossians 3:22–24
  * Philippians 4:4–7
  * Romans 12:18–21

Preparation: Highlight the verses in the lesson you will reference during the session. You may want to write these references on the board so the students will have them when you mention them during the lesson. Find lesson handouts for participants, and a list of verses not referenced on their handouts, available online.

OVERVIEW
Lesson Objectives
- Living righteously doesn't mean we won't experience trials.
- Remembering who we are before God and that He is watching helps us to do the right thing.
- Living righteously allows God to bless us and others.
- Sometimes our trials are part of God's bigger plan for us and others.

Step 1   Begin the Lesson
- Pray—be sure to begin every lesson with prayer.
- Today we will introduce the story. Next meeting we will complete it.

Step 2   Set the Story
- The story of Joseph is in Genesis.
- Point to "The Bible Is Unique" handout, pages 21–23.

48

- Ask the question: "What kind of book is Genesis?" Historical
- Genesis is part of the Torah (also called the Pentateuch).
  - The first five books of the Bible
  - These are the books of Moses.
  - Beginning of God's interaction with man
  - Beginning of His building the nation of Israel

Step 3 Summarize the Beginning of Joseph's Story—Genesis 37

- Look at verse 2. Ask the following questions: (Optional: have students underline answers in their Bibles.)
  - How old is Joseph? **17**
  - Who is his father? **Jacob**
  - What is Joseph's job? **shepherd** tending the flocks.
- Verse 4 tells us his brothers hated him. Have the students skim verses 2–4. Ask, "Why did the brothers hate Joseph?"
  - He **told on** them.
  - Their father **loved** Joseph **more**.
  - Their father gave him a **special robe** that was richly ornamented, "a many-colored robe." This robe marked Joseph as special.
- Read Genesis 37:5–11. God gave Joseph two dreams that indicated he would rule over his family. Ask, "How do you think they felt about that?" (See verse 11.)
  - His brothers were **jealous**.
  - His father **kept it in mind**.

DISCUSS THE FOLLOWING

Have the students predict what might happen to Joseph.

- Briefly summarize Genesis 37:12–36 for the students.
  - Joseph's brothers are out pasturing the flocks some distance away. Jacob sends Joseph to check on them. (verses 12–14)
  - The brothers see him coming. How do they treat him? (verses 18–20)
    - They decide to kill him. (verse 20)
  - The oldest brother persuades them not to kill Joseph but to throw him into a cistern (a well) so he can rescue Joseph later. (verses 21–22)
  - They remove his robe, throw him into the empty well, and sit down to eat. (verses 23–25)
    - Genesis 42:21 says that Joseph pleads for his life with his brothers.

- So they are eating lunch while he is crying out to them for his life.
  - Say, "How insensitive! Imagine."
- They see a caravan of traders coming. What idea do they get next?
  - They decide to sell him. (verses 26–27) Whose idea was this? Judah's
  - They tear up his robe, put blood on it, and tell their father that Joseph is dead. (verses 31–32)
- Jacob mourns for Joseph a long time. (verse 34)
- In the meantime, Joseph is sold to an Egyptian named Potiphar, the captain of the guard. (verse 36)
- Say, "That is how Joseph ends up in Egypt. Let's see what he does there and how he reacts to what has happened to him."

Step 4   Joseph in Potiphar's House—Genesis 39:1–6

- Read Genesis 39:1–6. Ask and discuss the following questions:
- Do you think Joseph was where he wanted to be?
  - **No**, he probably wanted to be home as the preferred son of his father.
- How might Joseph have reacted?

  - **Angry**
  - **Rebellious**
  - **Violent**
  - Students may come up with other reactions.
- What was different about Joseph? Have your participants underline the following:
  - Verse 2: "The Lord was with Joseph and he prospered."
  - Verse 3: "The Lord was with him" and "the Lord gave him success in everything he did"
- Who noticed?
  - **Potiphar** (verses 3–4)
- What did he do?
  - Put him **in charge of everything** (verse 4)
- What did God do?
  - **Blessed** Potiphar because of Joseph (verse 5)
  - In the New Testament, Peter urges us to live such godly lives that, though some accuse us of wrong, they will see our good deeds and glorify God (1 Peter 2:12).
  - Isaiah 61:8–9 makes a similar point.

Step 5 More Trouble in Joseph's Life—Genesis 39:7–20

- Read 39:7–20. Ask and discuss the following questions:
  - Did Joseph do anything to bring this trouble on himself? <u>No</u>
  - What was he doing? <u>**Being a faithful servant (verses 8–9)**</u>
  - How did he respond to Potiphar's wife's offer? <u>**Said it would be "against God" (verse 9)**</u>
  - Joseph was Potiphar's slave, but who was he really serving? <u>**God**</u>

★ Application to Life

Read Colossians 3:22–24, in the New Testament. It says slaves and masters but we can substitute any relationship where others have authority over us—employer, teacher, parent.

Who is our real audience? <u>God</u>

Where will our real reward come from? Read Ephesians 6:5–9.
The reward comes from God. (verse 8)
This passage describes Joseph.
He did what was right and not only when Potiphar was looking.
He knew it was God he was serving, and God is always looking.

Notice, Joseph was living a righteous life, but this did not keep the trials away.
Can this happen to us? Why does it happen?

What hope is there for us? Read John 16:33.
Jesus did not promise we would escape all troubles.
In fact, He promised we would have trouble, but that He gives peace.

Read Matthew 28:20 and Hebrews 13:5.
Jesus promises to be with us.

Step 6 Joseph in Prison

- Ask, "Where is Joseph now?"
  - <u>**In prison**</u> Genesis 39:20
- Read 39:21–23.
- Ask, "What is Joseph doing?" Have the students underline the following:

- Verses 21, 23: God is still with him.
- Verse 22: The warden put him in charge, again.
- Verse 23: The Lord gave him success.

★ Application to Life

How should we behave when we are going through trials?

Scripture offers hope and instruction for times when we go through trials.

Read and discuss Philippians 4:4–7; 12–13; and Romans 12:18–21.

Step 7 Summary

- Joseph was living a righteous life, but trials kept coming.
- Joseph continued to do the right thing because he knew who he was serving and who was watching.
- Living righteously blesses others. In Joseph's case, both Potiphar and the prison warden were blessed.
- In the next lesson, we will see that God was working to bless not only Joseph and the people right around him. God planned to bless whole nations and, ultimately, the world through Joseph.

Step 8 Next Steps

★ Application to Life

If you know people who have faced a trial and yet have been faithful and found God to be faithful, invite them to give their testimony to your group (or if you have a testimony, share yours).

You can have the testimony given after this lesson or after the next lesson (Joseph, Part 2). Or you can have the testimony split into two parts. Set up the story of the trial this time as we have set up Joseph's trial, then show how God worked and was faithful to them after the next lesson where we see how God worked in Joseph's life.

A woman who has given a testimony like this doesn't call it "my testimony." She calls it "God's testimony" because she considers it a testimony to God's faithfulness. She knows that the outcome wasn't due to anything she did or deserved.

- Pray.

The Beginning of Joseph's Story

How old is Joseph? **17** Genesis 37:2

Who is his father? **Jacob**

What is Joseph's job? **shepherd**

Why did his brothers hate Joseph? Genesis 37:2–4

- He **told on** them.
- Their father **loved** Joseph **more**.
- Their father gave him a **special robe**.

When Joseph told his dreams, how did his family feel about that? Genesis 37:11

- His brothers were **jealous.**
- His father **kept it in mind.**

Joseph in Potiphar's House—Genesis 39:1–6

Do you think Joseph was where he wanted to be? **No**

How might Joseph have reacted?

- **Angry**
- **Rebellious**
- **Violent**

Who noticed? **Potiphar** Genesis 39:3–4

What did he do? Put Joseph **in charge of everything**

What did God do? **Blessed** Potiphar Genesis 39:5

More Trouble in Joseph's Life—Genesis 39:7–20

Did Joseph do anything to bring this trouble on himself? **No**

What was he doing? **Being a faithful servant** Genesis 39:8–9

How does Joseph respond to Potiphar's wife's offer? Genesis 39:9

- Says it would be **against God**

Joseph was Potiphar's slave, but who was he really serving? **God**

Who is our real audience? **God**

Where is Joseph now? **In prison** Genesis 39:20

Joseph's Story, Part 2— Joseph in Pharaoh's House

Stepping Stones

> - Key Figure: Joseph
> - Key Word: Forgiveness
> - Key Concept: God initiates reconciliation with Himself by offering us forgiveness.
> - Key Scriptures: Genesis 40–45; 50:15–21
>
> - **Focal Verses**
>   - Joseph prospers. Genesis 41:39–49
>   - The brothers have changed. Genesis 44:14–34
>   - Joseph and his brothers. Genesis 45:1–15
>   - Joseph's father dies. Genesis 50:15–21
>
> - **Related verses**
>   - Philippians 2:12–13
>   - Isaiah 50:10–11
>   - Hebrews 11:1
>   - Romans 8:24–25

Materials needed: "Voice of Truth" CD and words handout, CD player or have on hand a copy of a hymn, such as "When We Walk with the Lord" or "Faith Is the Victory." Find lesson handouts for participants, available online.

Preparation: Highlight the verses in the lesson you will reference during the session. You may want to write these references on the board so the students will have them when you mention them during the lesson. Find lesson handouts for participants, as well as a list of verses not referenced on their handouts, available online.

OVERVIEW
Lesson Objectives

- To see that God has a plan for our lives even when we don't see it and times are hard.
- To see how Joseph offered his brothers complete forgiveness. He initiated it just as God does for us while we are still sinners.

Step 1   Begin the Lesson

- Pray—be sure to begin every lesson with prayer.
- Today we will finish Joseph's story.

Step 2   Review Last Lesson

- Ask the following questions:
  - What book is the story of Joseph in?
    - Genesis
  - What kind of book is Genesis?
    - Historical
    - The story of the beginning of the Hebrew nation
  - Who was Joseph's father?
    - Jacob, who was later called Israel
  - What was his relationship with his brothers? Not good
    - They were jealous of him—Genesis 37:11
    - They hated him—Genesis 37:4
  - What did they do about it?
    - They sold him into slavery.
  - How did Joseph respond to this tragedy?
    - He lived a righteous life—Genesis 39:8–10
  - Whose approval did he seek?
    - God's—Genesis 39:9
  - Who was with him?
    - God—Genesis 39:2–3, 21, 23
  - What was the result?
    - He prospered—Genesis 39:2–3, 21, 23
    - He was put in charge—Genesis 39:4, 22
    - Others were blessed—Genesis 39:5, 23
  - However, he still faced trials.
    - Genesis 40:13–15—Joseph recounts his troubles to Pharaoh's cupbearer when he asks the cupbearer to help him get released. He notes that he has done nothing wrong to deserve the treatment he has received.
    - In John 16:33 Jesus assures us we will have trouble but that He has overcome the world.
- We left Joseph in prison, but his fortunes are about to turn around.

Step 3   Summarize Details—Joseph Prospers

- Two full years have passed while Joseph was in prison. Genesis 41:1
- Genesis 41—Pharaoh has **two dreams** that no one can **interpret**.
- Someone (the cupbearer) knows that Joseph interprets dreams. Genesis 41:9–13

- Joseph is brought before the Pharaoh. Genesis 41:14
- Joseph gives credit to God. Genesis 41:16
- Pharaoh tells Joseph his dreams. Genesis 41:17–24
- Genesis 41:25–36
    - Joseph **interprets** the dreams—seven years abundance, seven years famine.
    - He makes a **recommendation**—appoint someone to prepare for the famine. Genesis 41:33–36
- Pharaoh and the officials like the plan. Genesis 41:37
    - Joseph becomes Pharaoh's second-in-command in Egypt. Genesis 41:38–40
    - Joseph has just gone from the **prison** to the **palace**, from the bottom to the top.
- How much time has passed?
    - Look at Genesis 41:46. How old is Joseph now? **30 years old**
    - How old was he at the beginning of our story? **17 years old**—Genesis 37:2
    - How much time has passed? For **13 years** God's plan has continued to unfold.
    - Does Joseph know what God's plan is? **No**
    - How has he been behaving in the meantime?
        - **Trust and obey**
        - **Faith and faithfulness**
        - **Positive**
        - **Respect for authority**
- It happens as Joseph has predicted: **seven years abundance then famine**.

Week 3
Lesson 6
56

Step 4 Joseph's Brothers Appear in Egypt—Genesis 42:1–17

- Read Genesis 42:1–17.
- The famine didn't affect just Egypt. Who else do you suppose was affected by the famine? Joseph's family
    - Jacob sends his sons to Egypt to buy grain, but he does not send the youngest son, Benjamin. Genesis 42:1–4
        - Benjamin is the other son of Jacob's favorite wife and Joseph's only full brother.
    - The brothers **appear before Joseph**. Genesis 42:6–9
    - What does this remind you (and Joseph) of?
        - His **earlier dreams**
        - There are numerous other times in this story where they will pay homage to Joseph. Genesis 42:6; 43:26, 28; 44:14; 50:18
- Joseph recognizes his brothers, but they don't recognize him.

- This is the moment Joseph has waited for: a **reunion** with his family. What choices does he have now?
  - **Joy—at being reunited**
  - **Vengeance—he has the power and means to take it**.
- We find out later that Joseph is glad to be reunited, but he is wary.
  - How did he last leave his family? He was sold into slavery.
  - He wants to know if anything has changed.
  - He tests his brothers.

Step 5   Joseph Tests His Brothers—Genesis 42–44

- Joseph **tests** his brothers without revealing himself to see if they are the same selfish and murderous men who sold him. He wants to know if they would sell out a brother again.
- Briefly summarize how Joseph tests his brothers. Genesis 42:17 to 44:12
  - Joseph puts them all in prison for three days. The roles have switched! Genesis 42:17
  - He tells them that one of them will stay behind and the others will go back home with the grain.

  - They are to bring back their youngest brother to prove they are not spies.
  - Their **guilt** comes back to them. Genesis 42:21
  - Joseph has their sacks filled with grain and their money put back into their sacks.
  - On the way home they find the money in their sacks and they are afraid.
  - When they get home, they recount all that happened to them to Jacob, their father.
  - Jacob refuses to send Benjamin, the youngest, back.
  - The famine continues and Jacob tells his sons to go back to Egypt to get more grain.
  - Judah responds that they can't go back without Benjamin, and then he pledges himself as surety for Benjamin's safety. Jacob agrees and sends money and gifts with them. (Compare Genesis 37:26–27 to Genesis 43:8–9.)
  - The brothers arrive in Egypt, and Joseph invites them to his house for a meal. There he gives them gifts and asks about their father, but he does not reveal himself to them.
  - Joseph sends them home with grain and again has their money put in their sacks. He also has his silver cup put into Benjamin's sack of grain.
  - After they leave, Joseph sends his steward after them to accuse them of stealing. The steward brings them back to Joseph.
- Read Genesis 44:14–17.
  - Joseph confronts them and they offer themselves as his slaves, but Joseph says he only wants the one who had the cup.

- Joseph's tests have singled out Benjamin.
  - The youngest—the other favorite of their father
  - The brother that Jacob didn't want to send back because he was afraid to lose him
  - Joseph's full brother—the only other son of Jacob's favorite wife Genesis 44:20, 28–29
- They call themselves his slaves—again the roles have switched! Genesis 44:16
- Joseph is threatening to keep Benjamin and send the rest of the brothers back to Jacob without him. Genesis 44:17

DISCUSS THE FOLLOWING
Read Genesis 44:18–34. What is different this time?
• **Judah offers himself in Benjamin's place.** • Last time it was his idea to sell Joseph. Genesis 37:26–27 • He is protecting Benjamin and Jacob. • Judah fulfills a promise he made to Jacob when the brothers left to go back to Egypt. Genesis 43:8–10
The brothers have **changed**. They **pass** the test.

Week 3
Lesson 6
58

Step 6   Forgiveness and Reconciliation
- Joseph initiates a new relationship with his brothers.
  - Read Genesis 45:1–8.
  - Joseph makes himself known to his brothers. Genesis 45:3
  - They are terrified; this powerful man is the brother they tried to kill long ago.
  - Notice that even though Joseph was the wronged party, he initiates **reconciliation**. He is offering forgiveness and wanting to restore the relationship with his brothers. Genesis 45:4–8
  - He is comforting them, saying, "It's OK; I forgive you."
- Joseph offers lavish forgiveness.
  - Read Genesis 45:9–15.
    - He could have sold them the grain and then said, "Come back anytime you need grain."
    - Instead, Joseph tells them to **move everything to Egypt**; he will take care of it all. Genesis 45:9–11
    - He hugged, wept, and kissed all his brothers, not just his favorite brother. Genesis 45:14–15
      - It was not just a pat on the back.

★ **Application to Life**

Here Joseph shows us what **God is like.**

This is how God loved us when we were still sinners. Romans 5:6–8.

God initiates this process of forgiveness and restoration with us even though He is the wronged party. He did not wait for us to ask for forgiveness before He sent Jesus and began calling us back to Himself.

This is also important for us when we are wronged. If we are to be like Christ, we must initiate restoration also, as Joseph did.

Step 7   God Had a Plan

- Have students skim Genesis 45:5–9. Tell them to look for and underline the repeating phrase or idea.
  - In these five verses, Joseph says "God sent me" or "made me" five times!
  - Note that this has the idea that God caused it to happen, but not that God forced Joseph.
- God had a **plan and purpose** for sending Joseph to Egypt.
  - Through Joseph's obedience, God saved lives (Genesis 45:5)—not just the lives of Joseph's family, but also of the Egyptians and the people in surrounding nations that were also affected by the famine. Joseph would have been OK if this was the only plan.
  - But it wasn't the only plan. God had more in mind. He was **preserving** the family of Abraham, which is the family that God has made promises to and the family that will ultimately bring forth the Savior (Messiah)—Jesus.
    - Joseph's brothers wanted to take his life, but God used that to save their lives (Genesis 45:7).
    - This foreshadows Jesus. His "brothers"—the Jews—also took His life, but God used that to bring salvation to the whole world.
  - As with many of the prophecies, God had an immediate effect in mind and an ultimate fulfillment through Jesus Christ.

★ **Application to Life**

How do we apply the lessons we learn from Joseph's life?
Read and discuss the following verses.
- Romans 8:28 says that God causes all things to work together for good. That includes things that in themselves do not seem good.
- Jeremiah 29:11 says "I know the plans I have for you." God has a plan for each of us.

- Isaiah 55:8–9 says "My thoughts are not your thoughts." Sometimes when God is working out His plan, as in Joseph's life, it doesn't seem good, but He knows things we don't know and He has plans that we don't know about.

What do we do during the trials?

Realize that God is in control—even when things don't make sense.

When all is dark, we need to walk in faith (trust). Faith is for when it is dark.

- Hebrews 11:1 says faith is being sure of what is hoped for and certain of what is *not* seen.
- Isaiah 50:10–11 says that those who walk in the *dark* should trust the Lord, but those who light their own fires (meaning they won't trust the Lord, but decide to make their own way) will lie down in torment.
- In Psalm 23:4 David says that even though he walks through the valley of the shadow of death, he does not fear because he knows God is with him.

Have students turn to Philippians 2:12–13, which says, "work out your salvation with fear and trembling, for God works in you to will and to act according to His good purpose."

- This shows the balance between what God does and what we do.
- "Work out" means to live out our salvation even trusting God in the bad and in the dark.
- Verse 13 shows why. God has a purpose in everything. Sometimes God allows us to see His purpose; sometimes He doesn't.

How do we treat others who have wronged us?

Even though God used it, the mistreatment by his brothers created much distress in Joseph's life. However, when he had the reason, the chance, and the means to retaliate, he offered forgiveness to them instead. This is how God treats us. See Romans 5:6-8.

Step 8 Joseph's Brothers Never Really Understood His Forgiveness

- Read Genesis 50:15–21.
  - Time has passed and Jacob, their father, has died. The brothers are back to their old mind-set (worrying and making up stuff). Genesis 50:15–17
    - For believers, it should not be like this. Second Corinthians 5:17 says that when we are in Christ we become a new creature, the old has gone.
  - It hurt Joseph that his brothers did not trust his forgiveness. Genesis 50:17b
    - Do we do this to God?

- In Genesis 50:18, Joseph's brothers bowed again. This is the fifth time in Joseph's story that they have done this. Remember Joseph's dreams in Genesis 37? The brothers didn't think they would ever bow to Joseph and even his father had his doubts, and yet the brothers have bowed repeatedly since they encountered him in Egypt, thus fulfilling God's revelation to Joseph.

Step 9   Summary

- Genesis 50:19–21 summarizes it all.
  - Joseph reminds his brothers that God is in control—verse 19.
  - Joseph knows that God has had a purpose and a plan through it all—verse 20.
  - Joseph was lavish with his forgiveness of his brothers—verse 21.
- Joseph was faithful through it all, even in the difficult times when he didn't understand what God was doing.

Step 10   Next Steps

- Invite someone to finish or to give their testimony as suggested at the end of Lesson 5. See Lesson 5 for details.
  - What I tell you in the dark, speak in the light. Matthew 10:27
- Play the song "Voice of Truth" by Casting Crowns. You may want to find the words on the Internet and pass them out so the students can follow along.
  - Or sing a hymn such as "When We Walk with the Lord" or "Faith Is the Victory."
  - Pray.

HANDOUT KEY: LESSON 6—JOSEPH'S STORY,
PART 2—JOSEPH IN PHARAOH'S HOUSE

Joseph Prospers

Pharaoh has **two dreams** that no one can **interpret.**

Joseph **interprets** the dreams and makes a **recommendation.**

Joseph goes from the **prison** to the **palace.**

How old is Joseph now? **30 years old** Genesis 41:46

How old was he at the beginning of our story? **17 years old** Genesis 37:2

How much time has passed? **13 years**

Does Joseph know what God's plan is? **No**

How has he been behaving in the meantime?

- **Trust and Obey**
- **Faith and Faithfulness**
- **Positive**

- **Respect for authority**

It happens as Joseph predicted: <u>**seven years abundance then famine**</u>.

Joseph's brothers <u>**appear before him in Egypt.**</u> Genesis 42:6–9

What does this remind you (and Joseph) of? His <u>**earlier dreams**</u>

This is what Joseph has waited for: a <u>**reunion**</u> with his family.

What choices does Joseph have now?
- <u>**Joy — at being reunited**</u>
- <u>**Vengeance — he has the power and means to take it**</u>.

Joseph <u>**tests**</u> his brothers.

Their <u>**guilt**</u> comes back to them. Genesis 42:21

Joseph is threatening to keep the youngest brother in Egypt. What is different this time? Genesis 44:18–34: <u>**Judah offers himself in Benjamin's place**</u>.

- The brothers have <u>**changed**</u>. They <u>**pass**</u> the test.
- Joseph initiates <u>**reconciliation**</u>. Genesis 45:4–8
- He tells them to <u>**move everything to Egypt**</u>. Genesis 45:9–11
- Joseph shows us what <u>**God is like.**</u>

- God had a <u>**plan and purpose**</u> for sending Joseph to Egypt. Genesis 45:5
- He was <u>**preserving**</u> the family of Abraham, which is the family that God has made promises to and the family that will ultimately bring forth the Savior (Messiah) — Jesus.

How do we apply the lessons we learn from Joseph's life?

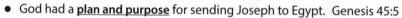

_____

_____

_____

_____

_____

_____

_____

_____

_____

_____

Moses's Story, Part 1— Moses's Life story

Stepping Stones

> ➢ Key Figure: Moses
> ➢ Key Word: Faithful
> ➢ Key Concept: God keeps His promises.
> ➢ Key Bible Books: Exodus, Leviticus, Numbers, Deuteronomy

Materials Needed: *The Prince of Egypt* video or some other video about the life of Moses (optional). Find lesson handouts for participants, available online.

OVERVIEW
Lesson Objectives
- To get an overview of Moses's life.
- To see a little about Moses's character and personality.
- To see how God begins to fulfill His promises to Abraham through Moses.

Step 1 Begin the Lesson
- Pray—be sure to begin every lesson with prayer.
- Today we will begin Moses's story.

Step 2 Review Last Lesson
- Ask the following questions:
  - In what books of the Bible is Moses's story found?
    - Exodus, Leviticus, Numbers, Deuteronomy
    - These are all books of history.
    - They are the last four of the five books of Moses (Torah, Pentateuch).
    - These books contain the accounts of Israel leaving Egypt and God giving the Law.
  - Where did we leave Joseph and the Israelites?
    - In Egypt
    - Before dying, Joseph asked them to bring his bones with them when they returned to the land God had promised to Abraham. Genesis 50:25

63

Step 3   Set Up the Beginning of Moses's Story

- Time has passed—about 400 years.
  - This was in accordance with a promise God made to Abraham in Genesis 15:13–14. Here God had told him that his people would be strangers in a country not their own and that they would be enslaved for 400 years. Then they would return.
  - In Exodus 12:41 we will see that God has kept that promise and Israel will leave Egypt.
- In Exodus 1 we learn that during that time, Jacob's (Israel's) family has grown, but the political climate in Egypt has also changed.
  - Seventy people had come to Egypt.
  - They multiplied greatly. By some estimates there are now about 2.5 million Israelites in Egypt.
  - A new king arises who does not know Joseph.
  - He is afraid of the Israelites (especially their great number) and enslaves them.
  - In order to control their population, Pharaoh tells the midwives to kill the Israelite baby boys. They don't because they feared God.
- In Exodus 2 God begins to do a new thing. A special child is born to a special family.

Step 4   Discuss, Tell, Watch Moses's Story

- Moses lived 120 (mostly) eventful years. His story appears in the last four books of the Torah (Exodus, Leviticus, Numbers, Deuteronomy).
- The Summary of Moses's Life Handout (printed below and available online) summarizes the details of his life. You could give this handout to the students and use it to highlight some events by reading and discussing the Scriptures where his story appears. You can use the Questions and Answers Handout as you review Moses's life story.
- You may want to focus on the following:
  - His birth and miraculous rescue
  - His early life in Pharaoh's palace
  - His attempt to rescue Israel using his own influence
  - God's humbling of him for 40 years as a shepherd far from the palace in Egypt
  - God's calling and Moses's hesitation, excuses
  - His encounters with Pharaoh and the ten plagues
  - Israel's miraculous release from Egypt
- One idea for sharing Moses's life story is to dress up like Moses and tell the story firsthand.

- Make sure you are prepared. Read and reread the story of Moses so that you can tell it in a natural style and be clear about what details you will relate.
  - The Summary of Moses's Life Handout (printed below and available online) and the Moses Script (available online) can help you plan what details you will include.
  - If you need to refer to the Bible for details during your portrayal, you could say something about how long you lived and how long ago that was and tell them that you need help to remember by checking the autobiography that you wrote (i.e. the Torah).
  - Have fun, but be careful not to add anything to or take anything away from the Scripture. (Revelation 22:18–19)
  - You may want to give them the Summary of Moses's Life handout so they can follow along as you tell the story. Or you could pass it out at the end and use it to review the story.
- Or you could show a video of Moses's life, such as *The Prince of Egypt*, with the following warnings in mind.
  - Videos and books outside of the Bible may not follow the Bible carefully.
  - Often they add elements to make the story flow.
  - Sometimes the creators have another agenda they are putting forth.
  - Scripture is your standard. Make sure the video lines up with the actual story in the Bible. Or point out some places where the video strays from Scripture.
    - For example, Moses in *The Prince of Egypt* movie released in 1999 looks about 35 or 40 years old when he returns to Egypt, but he was actually 80 years old. (Exodus 7:7)

Step 5   Summary
- God keeps His promises.
  - God made many promises to Abraham.
  - In Moses's and Israel's story we see God fulfilling some of His major promises.
- Because Moses started out in Pharaoh's palace, he began with great advantages. He thought he should use those advantages to help his people, but God humbled him and showed him His plan.
- Even Moses was afraid to take on the task God was giving him, but God assured him that He would be with him.
- Moses faithfully followed God in leading Israel and has become a revered figure in Christianity, Judaism, and Islam.

Step 6   Next Steps
- Next lesson we will discuss how God used Moses to reveal Himself through the Passover, the Law, and the Tabernacle.
- Pray.

SUMMARY OF MOSES'S LIFE

Exodus 1: Israel after Joseph—time passes, about 400 years (Genesis 15:13–14; Exodus 12:41)

- Exodus 1:5   Seventy people came to Egypt.
- Exodus 1:7   They multiplied greatly.
- Exodus 1:8   A new king arose who did not know Joseph.
- Exodus 1:9–14   He is afraid of them and enslaves them.
- Exodus 1:15–17 He also tells the midwives to kill the sons, but they don't.

Exodus 2:1–9: Moses's birth—saved from death by his godly family

Exodus 2:10: Moses's training as son of Pharaoh's daughter

Exodus 2:11–22: Moses tries to help Israel—kills an Egyptian => 40 years in the desert as a shepherd

- "I did it my way."
- Moses has been humbled.

Exodus 2:23–25: God begins His plan.
- God heard, remembered, saw, took notice. => He is about to act.

Exodus 3:1–17 Moses encounters a burning bush in the desert. God wants Moses to lead His people. He is reluctant to take the task, and tries to get out of it, but God answers each excuse.
- Exodus 3:11–12 Moses—Who am I?
  - God—I will be with you.
- Exodus 3:13–15 Moses—Who are You?
  - God reveals His name—Yahweh; I AM Who I AM. Exodus 3:14
- Exodus 4:1–9 Moses—What if they don't believe me?
  - God gives Moses three miraculous signs.
- Exodus 4:10   Moses—I am not eloquent.
  - God — Who made man's mouth? I will help you and teach you what to say.
- Exodus 4:13   Moses—Please send someone else.
  - God—Aaron, your brother, will help you.

Exodus 4:19–22: Pharaoh will not let them go.

Exodus 4:21: God hardens Pharaoh's heart. This all happens to show God's glory.

Exodus 4:29–31: Moses and Aaron go to the Israelites.

Exodus 5–11: Moses and Aaron go to Pharaoh.
- 10 plagues—God shows that He is greater than any other god. Exodus 9:14
  - Exodus 7:20   Nile turns to blood; magicians copy

- Exodus 8:1–15   Frogs; magicians copy
- Exodus 8:16–19   Gnats; magicians can't copy, they recognize the "finger of God"
- Exodus 8:20–32   Insects; none on Israel
- Exodus 9:1–7   Livestock die; Israel spared
- Exodus 9:8–17   Boils; even magicians affected
- Exodus 9:18–35   Hail; those in shelter will be saved; none on Israel
- Exodus 10:1–20   Locusts; Pharaoh's servants beg him to relent
- Exodus 10:21–29   Darkness; Israel has light
- Exodus 11:1–10   Last plague—death of the firstborn

Exodus 12–14. Passover—God protects Israel from the last plague; foreshadows the Cross.

- Exodus 12:1–13 & Exodus 12:21–28   Passover Lamb
- Exodus 12:14–20   Unleavened Bread
- Exodus 12:29–30   Angel of Death
- Exodus 12:42–51   To be observed forever

- Israel Leaves Egypt
  - Exodus 12:31–32   Pharaoh lets them go.
  - Exodus 12:33–36   Israel plunders the Egyptians, as promised by God (Genesis 15:14; Exodus 3:21).
  - Exodus 12:37–41   Israel leaves Egypt.
  - Exodus 13:19   They take the bones of Joseph, as they promised him (Genesis 50:25).
  - Exodus 13:17–22   God leads them.
  - Exodus 13:21   Pillar of cloud by day; pillar of fire by night
- Red Sea
  - Exodus 14:1–12   Pharaoh pursues them; Israel is afraid.
  - Exodus 14:13–31   Red Sea parts. Israel crosses; Egypt is destroyed.
  - Exodus 15:1–21   Israel rejoices.

Exodus 15–40. Israel in the wilderness

- Murmur and Complain—a regular occurrence; Some examples below:
  - Exodus 15:22–27   Water (also Exodus 17:1–7)
  - Exodus 16:1–21   Manna (bread) and Meat
- The Law — Exodus 19–31
  - Exodus 20:1–17   The Ten Commandments
- The Tabernacle — Exodus 25–40
  - Exodus 25–31   God gives the design.
  - Exodus 35–40   The Tabernacle is constructed.

- The Golden Calf (Idolatry) — Exodus 32
  - Exodus 32:19–35   Moses breaks the tablets.
    The people are punished.
- Moses Sees God — Exodus 33:12–23
- God Replaces the Tablets — Exodus 34
  - Exodus 34:6–7   God describes Himself.

Leviticus — The Book of the Law

Numbers — More detail:
- Census, Laws, History
  - There are approximately 600,000 men counted in the census.
  - That means there are about 2.5 million people in total.
- The Promised Land
  - Numbers 13   They spy out the land. It is rich, but there are giants there.
  - Numbers 14:1–10   The people refuse to enter.
  - Numbers 14:20–25   They wander for 40 years—God's punishment.

Deuteronomy — Moses repeats the Law. (Deuteronomy means "second law".)
- Deuteronomy 34:5   Moses dies before Israel enters the Promised Land. In Numbers 20:8–13, Moses strikes a rock twice when God said to speak to the rock. As a result, God says Moses will not bring them into the land.
- Deuteronomy 34:6   God buried Moses; no one knows where the grave is.
- Deuteronomy 34:7   Moses was 120 years old and still strong.

HANDOUT KEY: LESSON 7—MOSES'S STORY, PART 1—MOSES'S LIFE STORY

Israel After Joseph
- Exodus 1:5: How many people came to Egypt with Jacob? **70 people in all**
Exodus 1:8: What happened that started trouble for the descendants of Jacob after Joseph died?
- **A new king who did not know about Joseph came to power.**
Exodus 1:11, 16: What did the new king do?
- **He enslaved them and killed the baby boys.**

Moses is born
Exodus 2:2, 10: How did Moses's mother save him from death?
- **She hid him in the Nile. Pharaoh's daughter found him and raised him as her son.**
Exodus 2:11–12: When he grew up, how did Moses try to help his people?

- **Killed an Egyptian who was beating a Hebrew slave**

Exodus 2:15: When the matter became known, what did Moses do?

- **He fled to Midian where he lived and worked as a shepherd for a long time (Exodus 2:23–3:1).**

God calls Moses.

Exodus 3:2: How did God get Moses's attention in the desert?

- **He called to him from a burning bush.**

God calls Moses, but Moses makes five excuses. What were they?

Exodus 3:11: Moses's first question:

- **"Who am I, that I should go to Pharaoh and bring the sons of Israel out of Egypt?"**

Exodus 3:12: God's response:

- **He would be with Moses and give him a sign — Moses and the people would worship on the mountain where he was standing.**

Exodus 3:13: Moses's second question:

- **"What if the Israelites asked him, 'What is His (God's) name?' Then what shall I tell them?"**

Exodus 3:14–15: God's response:

- **God told Moses His Name**
- **I AM Who I AM. . . . This is my name forever."**

Exodus 4:1: Moses's third question:

- **"What if they don't believe me?"**

Exodus 4:8: God's response:

- God gave him **three** signs.
  - **Stick turned into a snake and back into a stick.**
  - **His hand turned leprous when he put it in his cloak and then changed back when he put it in his cloak again.**
  - **Water from the Nile turned to blood when he poured it out.**

Exodus 4:10: Moses's fourth excuse:

- **"O LORD, I have never been eloquent."**

Exodus 4:11–12: God's response:

- **"Who gave man his mouth? . . . Is it not I, the LORD? Now go; I will help you speak and will teach you what to say."**

Exodus 4:13: Moses's last excuse:

- **"Please send someone else."**

Exodus 4:14: God's response:

- **God's anger burned against Moses, and He told him that his brother, Aaron, was on his way and would help him.**

Moses and Aaron Go to Pharaoh

Moses and Aaron go to Pharaoh to ask him to release the people of Israel, but he refuses. Then God sent a series of ten plagues on Egypt. What were they?

Exodus 7:20	**Nile turns to blood**
Exodus 8:3	**Frogs**
Exodus 8:16	**Gnats**
Exodus 8:21	**Insects**
Exodus 9:3	**Livestock die**
Exodus 9:9	**Boils**
Exodus 9:18	**Hail**
Exodus 10:4	**Locusts**
Exodus 10:21	**Darkness**
Exodus 11:5	**Last plague — death of firstborn**

- Exodus 12. For the last plague, how did the Lord protect the Israelites? **Passover**

Pharaoh Lets Israel Go

When Pharaoh let Israel go, what did they take with them?
- Exodus 12:35–36: **They plundered the Egyptians; the Egyptians gave them gold, silver, and clothing.**
- Exodus 13:19: **The bones of Joseph as promised to Joseph — Genesis 50:25**

Exodus 13:21: How did God lead Israel when they left Egypt?
- **Pillar of cloud by day; pillar of fire by night**

Exodus 14:9: When Pharaoh realized he had let all his slaves go, what did he do?
- **Pursued them with horses and chariots and troops**

Exodus 14:10: When Israel saw Pharaoh and his army, how did they respond?
- **They were terrified and cried out to the Lord.**

Exodus 14:29–30: How did God save Israel?
- **He parted the Red Sea so they could walk across on dry land.**
- **The sea returned and the Egyptian army drowned.**

Israel Reaches the Promised Land — The First Time

Numbers 14:1–4: How did Israel react when they reached the Promised Land and found out there were giants living in the land?

- **They rebelled and wanted to return to Egypt.**

Numbers 14:29, 34: How did God respond?

- **He said they would wander for 40 years until all the generation who rebelled was dead.**

Moses Dies

Moses died before Israel entered the Promised Land (Deuteronomy 34:5).

- Deuteronomy 34:5–6: Who buried him? **God**
- Deuteronomy 34:7: How old was Moses when he died? **120 years old**

Moses's Story, Part 2— Passover, the Law, the Tabernacle

Stepping Stones

> Key Figure: Moses
> Key Word: Revelation
> Key Concept: God reveals Himself.
> Key Bible Books: Exodus, Leviticus, Numbers, Deuteronomy

OVERVIEW
Lesson Objectives

- To see how God reveals Himself through the Passover, the Law, and the Tabernacle.
- To see some ways these revelations are fulfilled by Jesus Christ in the New Testament.

Step 1   Begin the Lesson
- Pray—be sure to begin every lesson with prayer.
- Today we will finish Moses's story by looking at how God used him to reveal Himself through the Passover, the Law, and the Tabernacle.

Step 2   Review Last Lesson
- What books of the Bible is the story of Moses in? Exodus, Leviticus, Numbers, Deuteronomy — books of history
- Remind them that the last lesson discussed Moses's life story.
- Remind them of which events you discussed or ask them to recount some of the highlights of Moses's life.
- Ask if they have any questions about his life.

★ Teacher's Note

The Moses's Story, Part 2 Handout closely follows this teacher outline. The students will be able to follow and take notes on their handouts.

Step 3   The Passover
- The Passover was instituted in the Old Testament.

- From the beginning of time God has been saying to men, "There is no way to approach me except by coming with a lamb."
- After Adam and Eve sinned, they tried to cover themselves with fig leaves Genesis 3:7 But **God sacrificed an animal "to cover" their sin.** Genesis 3:21
- **Abel's sacrifice of the firstlings of his flock was accepted, but Cain's sacrifice of the fruit of the ground was rejected.** Genesis 4:3–5
- Read Exodus 11–12 together. (Exodus 11:4–10; 12:1–14, 21–28)
  - Exodus 11–12 **describes the Passover instituted to protect Israel from the last of the ten plagues against Egypt.**
  - God said they were to observe this event as a permanent ordinance for them and their children forever. Exodus 12:14, 24
  - When their children asked what it meant, they were to say, "It is the Passover sacrifice to the Lord, who passed over the houses of Israelites in Egypt and spared our homes when he struck down the Egyptians." Exodus 12:26–27
- The Law
  - God made it clear that sin must be paid for by blood. (Hebrews 9:22)
  - Animals are the substitutes.
- The Prophets
  - They showed God's people that sacrifice was not to be just a ritual, but from the heart.
  - Isaiah 53 introduces the Lamb to replace lambs. Jesus fulfilled this very detailed passage through His life and death on the Cross.
- The Passover was fulfilled in the New Testament.
  - When Abraham was told to sacrifice his son Isaac, Isaac asked, "Where is the lamb for the burnt offering?" Abraham answered, **"God himself will provide the lamb for the burnt offering, my son"** (Genesis 22:7–8). But for Isaac's sacrifice, God provided a ram caught in the thicket by his horns (Genesis 22:13). In John 1:29, 36 **when he sees Jesus approaching, John the Baptist answers the question that Isaac asked, "Behold, the Lamb of God who takes away the sin of the world!"**
  - Other New Testament writers also identify Jesus as the Lamb of God. Some samples:
    - Paul in 1 Corinthians 5:7
    - Peter in 1 Peter 1:18–19
    - John in Revelation 5:6; 13:8
  - The Last Supper (Passover) that Jesus celebrates with His disciples before He is crucified becomes the Lord's Supper (Communion).
    - This is my body and blood of the new covenant . . . for forgiveness of sins. (Matthew 26:26–29; Mark 14:22–25; Luke 22:14–20)

- Both the Passover and the Lord's Supper happened before the event they were to commemorate had transpired.
  - It is still a memorial today.
  - Luke 22:19 says, "Do this in remembrance of me."
  - 1 Corinthians 11:23–26 says, "until he comes again."
- Look over some of the comparisons between the Passover Lamb and Jesus using the handouts.

Step 4   The Law and the Ten Commandments
- Briefly discuss details about the Law.
- The Ten Commandments are part of the Law, and they summarize the basics of the Law.
- Work with the students to summarize each of the commandments using Exodus 20. Supply the following information for the notes:
  - 3rd commandment—Taking the Lord's name in vain does not just mean using it to curse. It is anything that defames or devalues God.
  - 4th commandment:
    - Applies to: **you, son, daughter, male and female servants, cattle, sojourner who stays with you.**
    - Reference to **Genesis 2:3: The Lord rested on the seventh day after He finished creating**.
  - 5th commandment promise: "**that you may live long in the land the Lord your God is giving you.**"

Step 5   The Tabernacle
- God lays out the requirements for the Tabernacle in Exodus chapters 25–31.
- His directions are very specific. Read Exodus 25:8–9; Hebrews 8:5.
  - How to raise the money
  - What it will look like
  - How it is to be oriented
    - Which direction it will face
    - Where it will be in relation to all the tribes in camp
  - Each piece of furniture
  - Materials to make everything with
  - Priests and their garments and their food
  - Tools and utensils
  - Sacrifices
  - Workmen—God even names two foremen.
    - Bezalel—Exodus 35:30
    - Oholiab—Exodus 35:34

- The Tabernacle is constructed.
  - The money is raised and all parts of the Tabernacle are made. Exodus 35–39
  - The Tabernacle is erected. Exodus 40:1–33
  - The cloud covers the tent and the glory of the Lord fills it. Exodus 40:34–38
- Point the students to the Handout of the Tabernacle design, based on The Kregel Pictorial Guide to the Tabernacle. If you can, have a 3-D model of the Tabernacle to show to the students.
- Discuss with them the significance of the different areas of the Tabernacle.
  - The Most Holy Place (Holy of Holies)
    - Contains the Ark of the Covenant
    - The curtain separating this area from the rest of the Tabernacle
  - The Holy Place
    - The Altar of Incense
    - The Seven-Branched Lampstand
    - The Table of the Bread of the Presence
  - The Laver (washstand)
  - The Altar of Sacrifice
  - Note that the entrance faced east.
- Why so specific?
  - Much of it is symbolic.
  - It is a symbol of God's presence among us.
    - God was said to sit on the mercy seat of the Ark of the Covenant.
    - John 1:14 — The Word became flesh and made His dwelling among us.
      - Literal — The Word became flesh and tabernacled among us.
  - It is a picture of heaven.
    - Hebrews 8:1–6
      - Verse 2 says that Jesus is in "the sanctuary, the true tabernacle set up by the Lord, not by man."
      - Verse 5 says that the priests "serve at a sanctuary that is a copy and shadow of what is in heaven."
    - Hebrews 9:1–5 contains a description of the earthly Tabernacle.
  - On the Cross, Jesus Christ would fulfill the function of the Tabernacle and the sacrificial system.
    - Hebrews 9:11–12, 24–26 tells us that Christ entered the perfect Tabernacle (heaven) and brought the perfect sacrifice (His own blood).

Step 6   Summary

- The time Israel spent in the wilderness after they left Egypt was an important time in their history.
- Through Moses, God revealed much about Himself and how He would be approached by man.

- The Law was given to show His standards and to show us that we are sinful and separated from a holy God.
- The Passover and the Tabernacle show us God's grace. Even though we are sinful and separated from Him, He made a way for us to have our sins covered and for us to be reconciled to Him.
- All that God pictured in the Law and the sacrifices was fulfilled in Jesus Christ.

Step 7   Next Steps
- In the next two lessons we will discuss the life of Israel's greatest king, David.
- Pray.

HANDOUT KEY: LESSON 8—MOSES'S STORY,
PART 2—PASSOVER, THE LAW, THE TABERNACLE

Passover

Old Testament:

Necessity of animal sacrifice and blood to cover sins

Adam and Eve
- Genesis 3:7, 21 **God sacrificed an animal to "cover" their sin.**

Cain and Abel
- Genesis 4:3–5 **Abel's sacrifice of the firstlings of his flock was accepted, but Cain's sacrifice of the fruit of the ground was rejected.**

Abraham
- Genesis 22:7–8, 13 **"God himself will provide the lamb for the burnt offering, my son."**

Passover
- Exodus 11–12 **Describes the Passover instituted to protect Israel from the last of the ten plagues against Egypt.**

The Law — Sin must be paid for by blood. Animals can be substitutes.

The Prophets — Not just a ritual, but from the heart; Isaiah 53 the Lamb to replace lambs.

New Testament:
Jesus as the Lamb of God

John the Baptist
- John 1:29, 36 **When he sees Jesus approaching, John the Baptist answers the question that Isaac asked, "Behold, the Lamb of God who takes away the sin of the world!"**

Paul
1 Corinthians 5:7

Peter
1 Peter 1:18–19

John
Revelation 5:6, 13:8

The Passover—Last Supper—becomes the Lord's Supper, Communion
- Matthew 26:26–29; Mark 14:22–25; Luke 22:14–20
- It is still a memorial today. Luke 22:19; 1 Corinthians 11:23–26

Some of the comparisons between the Passover Lamb and Jesus

Passover Lamb	Jesus
Chosen (Exodus 12:5)	This is My Son in whom I am well pleased (Matthew 3:17).
Unblemished (Exodus 12:5)	Jesus knew no sin (2 Corinthians 5:21).
Examined (Exodus 12:6)	Jesus was questioned by enemies and passed every test.
Lamb was slain to save lives of Israel	Jesus was slain to save us from sin.
Blood on doorposts	Blood on our heart (figuratively)
Angel of death passes over Israel	God passes over us in judgment.
Bones not broken (Exodus 12:46)	The soldier does not break Jesus' legs (John 19:33–36).

The Law
- The Law is spelled out in
  - Exodus 19–31
  - Leviticus
  - Parts of Numbers
  - Parts of Deuteronomy
- Laws regulate the whole of Israelite society — worship, civil, moral, dietary, personal relationships, etc.
- God spells out how He will be approached and what it means to be righteous.
- God also foreshadows what He will do in Christ.

The Ten Commandments—Exodus 20:1–17
The first four commandments cover our relationship with God.

1. Exodus 20:3 <u>**You shall have no other gods before me**</u>.

2. Exodus 20:4–6 <u>**You shall not make for yourself an idol**</u>.

3. Exodus 20:7 <u>**You shall not misuse the name of the Lord**</u>.
   Note, this goes beyond <u>**cursing**</u>.

4. Exodus 20:8–11 <u>**Remember to keep the Sabbath day by keeping it holy**</u>.

   Note who it applied to: <u>**you, son, daughter, male and female servants, cattle, sojourner who stays with you**</u>.

   Note the reference to Genesis 2:3: <u>**The Lord rested on the seventh day after He finished creating**</u>.

The last six commandments cover our relationship with others.

5. Exodus 20:12 <u>**Honor your father and your mother**</u>.
   Note promise: <u>**"that you may live long in the land the Lord your God is giving you."**</u>

6. Exodus 20:13 <u>**You shall not murder**</u>.

7. Exodus 20:14 <u>**You shall not commit adultery**</u>.

8. Exodus 20:15 <u>**You shall not steal**</u>.

9. Exodus 20:16 <u>**You shall not give false testimony against your neighbor**</u>.

10. Exodus 20:17 <u>**You shall not covet**</u>.

The Tabernacle
Exodus 25–31. God begins to lay out the requirements for the Tabernacle
His directions are very specific.
Exodus 25:8–9; Hebrews 8:5

- How to raise the money
- What it will look like
- How it is to be oriented
  - Which direction it will face
  - Where it will be in relation to all the tribes in camp

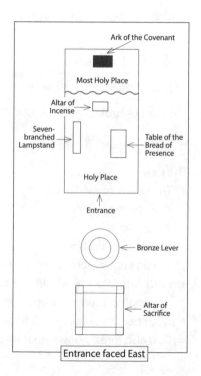

- Each piece of furniture
- Materials to make everything with
- Priests and their garments and their food
- Tools and utensils
- Sacrifices
- Workmen
- Even names two foremen:
  - Exodus 35:30—Bezalel
  - Exodus 35:34—Oholiab

Exodus 35–39 The money is raised and all parts of the Tabernacle are constructed.
- Exodus 40
  - 1–33   The Tabernacle is erected.
  - 34–38   The cloud covers the tent and the glory of the Lord fills it.

Why So Specific?
- Much of it is symbolic.
- It is a picture of heaven.
  - Hebrews 8:1–6
    - Verse 2 calls heaven the true Tabernacle the Lord pitched.
    - Verse 5 says the earthly Tabernacle is a copy and shadow of heavenly things.
  - Hebrews 9:1–5 description of the earthly Tabernacle
- Hebrews 9:11–12, 24–26 Christ, the perfect sacrifice brought into the perfect Tabernacle

David's Story, Part 1— The Man After God's Own Heart

Stepping Stones
> ➢ Key Figure: David
> ➢ Key Word: Heart
> ➢ Key Concept: David was a man after God's own heart.
> ➢ Key Scriptures: 1 Samuel 13:14; Acts 13:22; 1 Samuel 8; 9:15–7; 10:1; 13; 15–17; 24; 26; 2 Samuel 7; Psalm

Materials Needed: Copy of the song "The Majesty and Glory of Your Name." Look for a CD or play on the computer (optional). There are several versions available on YouTube.com. (There is a particularly good and clear one by MetroSingers.)

You may want to make a full set of handouts for students so they can follow along while the other groups report. Find lesson handouts for participants, available online. Just make sure they know which group they are in for group work so they complete the correct handout in the small groups.

Note: This is a long lesson. Begin promptly to give time for group work. Other options for teaching this lesson: pass out the handouts before this class and ask students to work on them ahead of time; choose one or two of the four possible events in David's life to discuss together as a class; consider extending the lesson to another session to have time for the groups to work together.

OVERVIEW
Lesson Objectives
- To look at some of the events of David's life to discover his character.
- Also look at some of the psalms where David worships and prays to God.

Step 1   Begin the Lesson
- Pray—be sure to begin every lesson with prayer.
- Today we will begin David's story by looking at his character and how God saw him.

Step 2   Review Last Lesson

- In the last lesson we looked at how God used Moses to reveal Himself through the Passover, the Law, and the Tabernacle, and how their purposes were fulfilled in the New Testament through Jesus Christ.
- The Passover was given to Israel to protect them from the last plague on Egypt, the death of the firstborn. It utilized the blood of a lamb sprinkled on the doorposts to make the Angel of Death "pass over" the houses of the Israelites. It foreshadowed what Jesus would do for us on the Cross. His blood on our hearts causes death to "pass over" us, thereby giving us eternal life.
- The Law was given to show Israel how they should approach God, how they should behave, and how they should treat one another. Included in the Law were consequences for disobedience. The main job of the Law was to show man's sinfulness. The Law did not save; it pointed out the need for a Savior (Romans 3:20).
- The Tabernacle was the visible presence of God in the camp of Israel. God gave very specific instructions about its layout and construction because it is a copy of the one in heaven. Jesus Christ fulfilled the purpose of the Tabernacle when He entered heaven itself with His own blood for the forgiveness of sin.

Step 3   Historical Setting of David's Story

- Look at "The Bible Is Unique" handout (pages 21–23) for Bible chronology.
  - Genesis through Deuteronomy are the five books of Moses. They contain the stories of the beginning of the nation of Israel through their release from slavery in Egypt.
  - The Book of Joshua tells the stories of Israel entering and conquering the Promised Land.
  - The Book of Judges contains a cycle of disobedience by the nation and correction by God.
  - The Book of Ruth is the story of King David's great-grandmother.
  - First and 2 Samuel detail the beginning of the monarchy and the story of David, Israel's greatest king.
  - David's full story starts in 1 Samuel 16 and continues through the Book of 2 Samuel and ends in 1 Kings 2:12. Parts of it are also told in 1 Chronicles. Some of his prayers are recorded in the Book of Psalm.
  - What kind of books are these? (See The Bible Is Unique.)
    - First and 2 Samuel, 1 Kings, and 1 Chronicles are books of history.
    - Psalm is a book of poetry. It is Israel's "songbook" for worship.

How God Sees David
- God considers David to be a man after His own heart.

- God told Samuel He had chosen a man after his own heart to rule Israel. 1 Samuel 13:14
- Paul quotes this verse when sharing the gospel in Pisidian Antioch on the first missionary journey. Acts 13:22

Step 4   **Look at Four Events in David's Life**

- Have the students look at four events in David's life that display his character.
- Form four groups. Each group will look at one significant event in David's life.
  - Samuel anoints David.
  - David kills Goliath.
  - David spares Saul's life — twice.
  - David plans to build a temple; God builds David a house.
- Have them use the handouts for this lesson to know which verses to look at and to help them discover facts about David's life.
- The handouts have many verses referenced, but the groups can limit themselves to reading only the verses needed to answer questions on their handouts. The other verses can serve as background information.

- Make yourself available to the groups and help them as needed.
- After they have had time to work in groups have them report to everyone.
  - What event is described?
  - What character quality does David display?
- See the handout key for suggested answers to the questions on the group handouts.

Step 5   **A Further Note on David's Character**

- David was a man of prayer and worship.
- Scholars attribute to David at least 73 out of the 150 psalms (about half).
- For an example, look at Psalm 8.
  - Have students skim Psalm 8 or, if you have time, read it together.
  - The words of this psalm were used in the beautiful song, "The Majesty and Glory of Your Name." If you have access to a copy, you could play it. There are several versions available on YouTube.com. (There is a particularly good and clear one by MetroSingers.)
- Encourage the students to skim some of the other psalms for more examples of how David prayed and worshipped. They will see that no subject or emotion was off-limits in his conversations with God.

Step 6   **Summary**

- God considered David to be a man after His own heart.
- David proved he was worthy of this name in his actions.

Step 7 Next Steps

- In the next lesson, we will see that David was still a man capable of sin.
- We will see how he sins and how God restores him.
- Pray.

HANDOUT KEY: LESSON 9—DAVID'S STORY, PART 1—THE MAN AFTER GOD'S OWN HEART

Group 1: Samuel Anoints David—1 Samuel 16:1–13
Background

- By the Law, God had set up Israel as a theocracy with Himself as their head.
- 1 Samuel 8:19–20 After Israel had been in the Promised Land for a while, they asked for a king to rule over them so they would be like the other nations.
- 1 Samuel 8:10–18 It was not God's plan for them to be like the other nations, but He appointed a king over them with many warnings about what a king would do to them.
- 1 Samuel 9:15–17; 10:1 God chose Saul to be king over them.
- 1 Samuel 13:13–14; 15:26–29 Saul started out well, but then became disobedient, and God rejected him as king over Israel. Instead, God found a man after His own heart and appointed him as leader over Israel.

1. 1 Samuel 16:1–3 What did God send Samuel to Bethlehem to do?
   - Anoint the next king of Israel.

2. 1 Samuel 16:6 What did Samuel think when Jesse's oldest son, Eliab, stood before him?
   - Surely this is the one.

3. 1 Samuel 16:7 What did God say?
   - He is not the one.
   - Man looks on the outward appearance, but the Lord looks at the heart.

4. 1 Samuel 16:8–10 What did God say about Jesse's seven older sons?
   - He had not chosen them.

5. 1 Samuel 16:11 Where was David while these sons were passing before Samuel?
   - In the fields, tending the sheep

6. 1 Samuel 16:12 What did God say when David was brought before Samuel?
   - Anoint him; he is the one.

7. Why didn't the family call David in from the fields to be looked at by Samuel?
   - They considered him the youngest and least important member of the family.

8. What were Samuel and the family looking at?
   - Outward appearance (family status, qualifications, etc.)

9. What was God looking at?
   - The heart — in David, God found a man after His own heart.

Group 2 : David Kills Goliath—1 Samuel 17:1–54
Background
King Saul and the Israelites were fighting the Philistines. The Philistines had a champion named Goliath who was over nine feet tall. Goliath proposed an alternative to battle — Israel could choose a man to fight him. The army of the loser would become the slaves of the army of the winner. Saul and his army were terrified. 1 Samuel 17:4–11

1. 1 Samuel 17:13–14 Which of Jesse's sons were fighting in this battle?
   - The three oldest — Eliab, Abinadab, Shammah

2. 1 Samuel 17:15 What was David doing during this time?
   - Going back and forth between Saul and returning to his sheep

3. 1 Samuel 17:16 How many days did Goliath come out and taunt the army of Israel?
   - 40 days

4. 1 Samuel 17:17–19 What did Jesse send David to do?
   - Take food to his brothers and bring back news of the battle

5. 1 Samuel 17:20–25 What did David see and hear when he came to the battlefield?
   - Army shouted and lined up for battle.
   - Goliath issued his challenge.
   - Israel ran in fear.
   - Saul promised a reward to anyone who would challenge Goliath.

6. 1 Samuel 17:26 What questions did David ask about the situation? How did he see it?

- What would be done for the man who killed this Philistine?
- A disgrace for Israel
- An uncircumcised Philistine defying the armies of the living God

David's brothers didn't like him asking questions, but David was overheard and it was reported to Saul. (1 Samuel 17:28–31)

7. 1 Samuel 17:32 David was brought before Saul. What did he offer to do for Saul?
   - Go out and fight Goliath

8. 1 Samuel 17:33–37 Saul didn't think it was a good idea. How did David reply? (verses 34–37)
   - I have killed lions and bears while tending sheep.
   - This Philistine will be like one of them.
   - He has defied the armies of the living God.
   - God will deliver me from him just like He delivered me from the lion and bear.

9. 1 Samuel 17:41–49 David and Goliath fought. Goliath insulted David. How did David respond? (verses 45–47)
   - I come against you in the name of the living God whom you have defied.
   - He will hand you over to me.
   - I will kill you.
   - The whole world will know there is a God in Israel.
   - God does not save by weapons.
   - The battle is the Lord's, and He will give you into our hands.

David killed Goliath and cut off his head. The Philistines ran away. Israel rejoiced and plundered the Philistine camp. David took Goliath's weapons as reward. 1 Samuel 17:50–54

10. For David, what was this battle really about?
    - The Philistines were defying the armies of the living God.
    - God would win this battle for Himself.

11. Who was fighting David's battles?
    - God

Group 3: David Spares Saul's Life Twice—1 Samuel 24; 26
Background
Saul was chosen as king of Israel, but he was disobedient and did not honor God. God rejected him from being king and chose another man, a man after His own heart, David. God removed His presence from Saul and began blessing David. Saul became jealous and looked for opportunities to kill David, but David kept avoiding capture. Twice David had an opportunity to kill Saul, but he did not.

David spares Saul's life in a cave.
- 1 Samuel 24:3–4 Saul was chasing David and took a break to relieve himself in a cave, the same cave where David and his men were hiding. What did David's men say? What did David do?
  - This is your chance. God has given him into your hands.
  - David cut off the corner of Saul's robe.
- 1 Samuel 24:5–7 David felt guilty for what he did. What did he say to his men?
  - God forbid that I do anything against my master or lift my hand against him.
  - He is the Lord's anointed.
  - He rebukes his men.

- 1 Samuel 24:8–15 After Saul left the cave, David came out and called to him. What did he say?
  - Why do you listen to others?
  - I had a chance to kill you and was encouraged to do so, but I did not.
  - I spared you because you are the Lord's anointed.
  - I am not guilty and have not wronged you.
  - May the Lord judge between you and me.
  - I will not touch you.
  - Who are you pursuing? A dead dog? A flea?
  - May the Lord deliver me from your hand.

David spares Saul's life in camp at night.
- 1 Samuel 26:5–8 Saul was chasing David and set up camp. David found out where Saul was and came into the camp at night with a few of his men. They got into the middle of the camp where Saul, his general, and his soldiers were sleeping. What did David's helper, Abishai, want to do? (verse 8)
  - God has delivered your enemy into your hands.
  - Let me pin him with one spear thrust.
- 1 Samuel 26:9–11 How did David reply?
  - No. Who can strike the Lord's anointed without guilt?
  - God will take care of it.

- I will not lay a hand on the Lord's anointed.
- He takes Saul's spear and water jug.
- 1 Samuel 26:12 Why were David and his men able to get into the middle of a camp of trained army men without being heard? Who was fighting David's battles?
  - God had put them into a deep sleep.

David taunted Saul's general for not protecting his king. 1 Samuel 26:13–16
- Saul heard and came out to talk to David. 1 Samuel 26:17–20
- Saul promised not to harm David. 1 Samuel 26:21
- David returned Saul's spear and reminded Saul that he spared his life. 1 Samuel 26:22–24
- Saul blessed David and they parted. 1 Samuel 26:25

1. What did David keep calling Saul?
   - The Lord's anointed

2. How did this affect David's behavior?
   - Respected God's choice
   - Waited for God to judge His own servant

3. Who was fighting David's battles?
   - God

4. Who was David relying on?
   - God

5. Whose plan was he following?
   - God's
   - Not his own

Group 4: David Plans to Build a Temple; God Builds David a House—2 Samuel 7

Background
David became king of Israel and united the people. He brought the Ark of the Covenant to Jerusalem, his capital city, with great rejoicing (2 Samuel 6).

1. 2 Samuel 7:1–3 God gave David rest from all his enemies. What did David tell Nathan, the prophet, that he wanted to do? What did Nathan reply?
   - David wanted to build a house for the ark.
   - Nathan said, "God is with you."

2. 2 Samuel 7:4–16 God spoke to Nathan in the night. In verse 7, what did He tell Nathan He had never asked for?
   - A house of cedar

3. 2 Samuel 7:8–9a What did God say He had done for David?
   - Brought you from flock to throne
   - Been with you wherever you have gone
   - Cut off all your enemies

4. 2 Samuel 7:9b–11 What did He promise to do for David?
   - Will make your name great, like the greatest men of the earth
   - Provide a place for My people
   - Wicked people would not oppress them anymore
   - Give him rest from all enemies
   - Establish a house for him

5. 2 Samuel 7:12–13 Who would build a house for the Lord?
   - David's descendant

6. 2 Samuel 7:16 What would God do for David's house?
   - Establish it forever

7. 2 Samuel 7:17 Nathan reported everything God said to David.
   2 Samuel 7:18–29 David prayed in response to all he had heard. What do you learn about David from this prayer?
   - He is humble
   - He is grateful
   - He is worshipful
   - David praises God for who He is and how He has treated Israel
   - Asks God to do what He has promised for His name and for David's
   - Finds courage to pray these prayers based on God's promises
   - Asks God to bless his house and make it last forever
   - States that because God has spoken, it will be so

8. How are these promises of an everlasting house ultimately fulfilled?
   Matthew 1:1
   - In Jesus, the Son of David

David's Story, Part 2—
The Man After God's Own Heart Sins

Stepping Stones

> - Key Figure: David
> - Key Word: Restoration
> - Key Concept: David sins and God restores.
> - Key Scriptures:

> **Background verses:**
>   - 2 Samuel 11–12:25
>   - Psalm 51
>   - Psalm 32

> **Focal verses:**
>   - 2 Samuel 11:1–27
>   - 2 Samuel 12:1–13
>   - Psalm 51:1–17
>   - Psalm 32

89

Preparation: Highlight in the lesson the verses you will reference during the lesson. Our students sometimes had trouble following the lesson because they were trying to get these references. It might be helpful to write these on the board so students will not miss anything while you are teaching. Find lesson handouts for participants, as well as a list of verses not referenced on their handouts, available online.

OVERVIEW
Lesson Objectives
- To see how even a man described as "a man after God's own heart" can sin.
- To see that, even so, this is not the end for him. God reaches out to restore him.

Step 1   Begin the Lesson
- Pray—be sure to begin every lesson with prayer.
- Today we will look at a dark chapter in David's life.
  - We will see what conditions set him up for a moral failure.
  - We will see how he dealt with his sin.
  - Then we will see how God dealt with his sin and how David responded.

Step 2 Review Last Lesson

- In the last lesson, what kind of man did we see that David was?
  - A man after God's own heart.
- Today we will see what happens when that man sins.
- The Bible is full of sinful people!
- We will see that David was called a man after God's own heart not because he was sinless, but because he always came back to seeking God.
- This story is in 2 Samuel. What kind of book is it? (See The Bible Is Unique.)
  - History

Step 3 The Setting for the Sin—2 Samuel 11:1

- Read 2 Samuel 11:1.
- What time of year is it? <u>spring</u>
- Where were the kings? going off to <u>war</u>
- Where was David? at <u>home</u> in Jerusalem
- David was not where he should have been or doing what he should have been doing.
  - What was the reason?
    - Not important
    - Maybe he forgot his duty or became complacent. Who knows?

★ Application to Life

Sometimes we make choices between a "good thing" versus a "God thing."

David wasn't necessarily doing anything wrong at this point, but we'll see that he set himself up for failure when he wasn't where he should have been.

Step 4 The Progression of Sin—2 Samuel 11:2–27

- Read 2 Samuel 11:2–27.
- Note the progression of sin. How did it start? It started with "David saw" and ended in premeditated murder.
  - In verse 2, David <u>saw</u> a woman bathing. This was an accident. There is no sin here. The sin begins with what David did next.
  - In verse 3, David <u>sent a messenger</u> to find out who she was. She was Bathsheba, the wife of Uriah the Hittite. David should have walked away at this point, but he didn't.
    - David knows Uriah personally. He is one of David's "mighty men" (2 Samuel 23:39).
  - In verse 4, David <u>sent for</u> the woman. She came to him and he <u>slept</u> with her, then she went home.

- In verse 5, she became pregnant and sent word to David. At this point, he began to try to **cover it up**. In verse 6 he sent for her husband, Uriah.
- After making small talk with Uriah, David sent him home hoping Uriah would sleep with his wife and later think the child was his (2 Samuel 11:7–9). However Uriah did not return home.
- David found out Uriah never went home and invited him to say stay one more day (2 Samuel 11:12). David made him drunk hoping he would go home to sleep with his wife, but again Uriah didn't go home (2 Samuel 11:13).
  - Uriah remembered his duty. He knew where he was supposed to be. He had more integrity than David.
    - o 2 Samuel 11:9: Uriah slept at the entrance to the palace.
    - o 2 Samuel 11:11: He refused to sleep with his wife while the rest of the army was in the field.
    - o 2 Samuel 11:13: He slept among his master's (David) servants.
- When David's plan didn't work, he sent Uriah back to the battlefield with a letter to the general (Joab) to put Uriah on the front lines (2 Samuel 11:15) and draw back from him. Uriah was traveling back with his own **death warrant.**
- Joab did as David requested and **Uriah died** (2 Samuel 11:17).
- David consoled Joab on the loss of a soldier but showed no remorse (2 Samuel 11:25).
- David knew better: Deuteronomy 17:14–20
  - Kings were not to take multiple wives.
  - A king was to write a copy of the law, keep it with him, and read it every day of his life. He was not to consider himself better than his brothers or turn from the Law to the right or left.
- David could have stopped at any point along the way.

★ Application to Life

Read James 1:13–15.
This passage details the progression of sin.
First, we are tempted. Note that we are not tempted by God.

- Temptation is not sin. Acting on temptation is sin.
- Jesus was tempted, but did not sin. Hebrews 4:15
- Sin happens when we make the wrong choice about the temptation.

Martin Luther once said, "You can't stop the birds from flying over your head. But you don't have to let them nest in your hair." What he meant is that we can't stop temptation from happening to us. Temptation comes to all of us and we can't stop that, but we don't have to give in to it. Sin happens when we give in to the temptation and commit the sin.

First Corinthians 10:13 assures us that God gives us a way out. We need to look for the way out when we are tempted.

Sin takes you **farther** than you want to go. It keeps you **longer** than you want to stay. It costs **more** than you want to pay. (*The Daily Hatch* attributes this quote to R. G. Lee.)

Step 5   Life Goes On or Does It? — 2 Samuel 11:26–27
- David and Bathsheba marry after her period of mourning.
- Some months later a child is born.
- They act like **nothing unusual** happened and **nobody knew**. This is not so.
  - Many messages had passed between the palace and Bathsheba's house.
  - Surely Joab was suspicious about the unusual command to put a man in harm's way and David's later lack of concern over his death.
- God was **displeased**. 2 Samuel 11:27 has an ominous sound to it, doesn't it?

★ Application to Life

God always sees and knows what we are doing, but He gives us free choice. (James 1:13–15 again)

Step 6   God Convicts David; He Repents and Is Restored—2 Samuel 12:1–14
- Read 2 Samuel 12:1–14.
- God always brings our **sin** to us. He **loves** us too much to leave us with it!
  - Proverbs 3:11–12 The Lord disciplines those He loves.
  - Hebrews 12:5–11 He disciplines us as a Father disciplines his sons (children).
    - If you are not disciplined, you are not a son.
    - Discipline is painful, but it produces a harvest of righteousness.
- The **Lord**, through **Nathan** the prophet, confronts David with his sin.
  - In 2 Samuel 12:1–4, Nathan tells David a **parable** (a word picture).
  - David thinks it is true and is angry (2 Samuel 12:5–6).
    - According to the Law, David is judge over his people, so he is doing his job here.
    - Exodus 22:1 says a man who steals a sheep must pay back four sheep.
  - But Nathan says, "You are the man!" (2 Samuel 12:7)
  - Nathan goes on to declare the message from God. (2 Samuel 12: 7–10)
    - God has already given David so much, and He would have given David more if it had not been enough.
    - He had killed Uriah, and he had despised the Lord.
- David's sin is forgiven, but choices still have consequences (2 Samuel 12:10–12).

If you followed the rest of David's story in the Bible, you would see that all these prophecies come true.

- The sword would never depart from his house.
- God would give his wives to someone close.
- What David did was in secret; God will do it openly.

- David **admitted** his sin against God and God **forgave** him. (2 Samuel 12:13)
  - This admission of guilt again shows David's **character,** which we studied last week. In these times, kings ruled supreme and did not have to answer to their people, but David is humble before God and His prophet.
  - By Law, David and Bathsheba both should have been put to death (Leviticus 20:10) but God, through Nathan, assures David that he will not die.
  - However, sin still has consequences: the child will die.
    - One reason for consequences is that sin causes others to stumble and makes the Lord's enemies show utter contempt. (2 Samuel 12:14)
  - But 1 John 1:9 says that if we confess our sins God is faithful to forgive and cleanse us from all unrighteousness.
- Deuteronomy 8:2 God tests us to show what is in our hearts, whether or not we will keep His commands.

★ Application to Life

In a very short time, David committed both adultery and murder, and then tried to cover it all up. But God did not let him stay in his sin. He brought it to David and gave him a chance to repent. David repented and was forgiven. However, there were still consequences from his sin.

God disciplines His children. He will do the same for us as He did for David.

Discuss with the students how this might work in our lives.

Step 7   How David Later Saw His Sin—Psalm 51 (and 32)

- Look at Psalm 51.
- Introductory notes to the psalm say, "For the director of music."
  - This psalm was to be sung at the Temple.
  - This is a very personal confession by the king to be sung publicly before all his subjects—unheard of for the time.
- In verse 4, David said "Against you, you only, have I sinned." Where have we seen this thought before?
  - Joseph, Genesis 39:9
  - David, 2 Samuel 12:13
  - Ultimately, **sin** is against **God,** who is righteous.

- In the English language, imperatives are a command or request, such as, "Come here," or, "Help me with this."
  - Have the group look for and underline these types of imperatives in Psalm 51:1–15.
- What does David ask God to do? Have the students tell you what they found. List their answers on a board at the front of the class.

Have mercy	Blot out my iniquity
Blot out transgressions	Create in me a clean heart
Wash away iniquity	Do not cast me away
Cleanse me from my sin	Restore joy to me
Cleanse me	Grant a willing spirit
Wash me	Save me from bloodguilt
Hide your face from my sins	Open my lips

- David is making a lot of requests of God. This is unexpected from a man who has just committed a great sin. Why does David think God will grant these requests?
  - Psalm 51:1 David says it is according to Gods' mercy, His unfailing love, His great compassion.

  - These attributes in Psalm 51:1 actually describe the character of God.
    - See Exodus 34:6–7.
    - In these verses God describes Himself.
    - Notice how similar this is to David's words.
    - David knew the Law and knew what God had said about Himself. David is asking for forgiveness on the basis of the **character of God as He has revealed Himself**.
- The word *love* in Exodus 34:6–7 and Psalm 51:1 is a very special word.
  - In Hebrew the word is *hesed*.
  - English does not have a single word that captures the meaning of this word. Some translations call it "loving kindness" or "unfailing love."
  - Its full meaning is **"covenant love."** It is based on the relationship God had with Israel through the covenants He had made with them through the patriarchs and Moses. It was based on His promises to them, not on their performance.
  - This is why David, even as a sinner, could boldly make requests of God.
  - Look again at what *kinds* of things David asked for. See the table you put on the board.
  - He is asking for **forgiveness and restoration**.
- What does God *not* want? Psalm 51:16
  - **Sacrifice**
- What *does* He want? Psalm 51:17
  - **A broken spirit**
  - **A broken and contrite heart**
- Summary: God wants humility and repentance, not sacrifices in an effort to appease Him.

- What are the results of restoration? Psalm 51:13–15
  - <u>I will teach transgressors your way.</u>
  - <u>Sinners will turn back to you.</u>
  - <u>My tongue will sing of your righteousness.</u>
  - <u>My mouth will declare your praise.</u>
  - All of this is what David is doing with this psalm as it was sung in the Temple before his people.

Step 8   Summary

★ Application to Life

Does being "a man after God's own heart" (or saved) mean we will never sin again? No

What happens when we sin?
- God confronts us. "You are the man!" 2 Samuel 12:7
- He disciplines us. "The child will die." 2 Samuel 12:13–14
- When we confess, He forgives and cleanses us. 2 Samuel 12:13; 1 John 1:9
- But there may still be consequences — the "sword will never depart from your house. . . . " 2 Samuel 12:10–12

What is the best response on our part when we sin?
- Confess our sin. 2 Samuel 12:13; Psalm 51:4; 1 John 1:9
- Rely on God's mercy and character. Psalm 51:1
- Don't just bring a sacrifice, but come with humility and repentance. Psalm 51:16–17

What are the results of restoration?
- We will have a testimony to share with others. Psalm 51:13
- We will praise God. Psalm 51:14–15

Step 9   Next Steps
- In the next lesson we will go to the New Testament and begin looking at the life of Jesus Christ who is the fulfillment of all the promises of God and of the Law and sacrificial system.
- Jesus said, "Do not think that I have come to abolish the Law or the Prophets; I have not come to abolish them but to fulfill them. I tell you the truth, until heaven and earth disappear, not the smallest letter, not the least stroke of a pen, will by any means disappear from the Law until everything is accomplished." Matthew 5:17–18
- Pray.

HANDOUT KEY: LESSON 10—DAVID'S STORY, PART 2—THE MAN AFTER GOD'S OWN HEART SINS

The Setting for the Sin—2 Samuel 11:1

What time of year is it? <u>spring</u>

Where were the kings? going off to <u>war</u>

Where is David? at <u>home</u> in Jerusalem

The Progression of Sin—2 Samuel 11:2–27

- David <u>saw</u> a woman bathing.
- David <u>sent a messenger</u> to find out who she was.
- David <u>sent for</u> the woman.
- David <u>slept</u> with her.
- David tries to <u>cover it up</u>.
  - Uriah was traveling back to the battle with his own <u>death warrant</u>.
  - Uriah <u>died</u>.
- David and Bathsheba act like <u>nothing unusual</u> happened and <u>nobody knew</u>.
- But God was <u>displeased</u>.

God Convicts David.—2 Samuel 12:1–14

- God always brings our <u>sin</u> to us. He <u>loves</u> us too much to leave us with it! (Proverbs 3:11–12; Hebrews 12:5–11)
- The <u>Lord</u>, through <u>Nathan</u> the prophet, confronts David with his sin.
- Nathan tells David a <u>parable</u>.
- David <u>admitted</u> his sin and God <u>forgave</u> him.
- This admission of guilt shows David's <u>character</u>.

How David Later Saw His Sin—Psalm 51 (and 32)

- Ultimately, <u>sin</u> is against <u>God,</u> who is righteous.
- David asks for forgiveness on the basis of <u>God's character as He has revealed Himself</u>.
- *Hesed* means "<u>covenant love</u>".
- David is asking for <u>forgiveness and restoration</u>.

What does God *not* want? Psalm 51:16 <u>Sacrifice</u>

What *does* God want? Psalm 51:17

- <u>A broken spirit</u>
- <u>A broken and contrite heart</u>

What are the results of restoration? Psalm 51:13–15

- <u>I will teach transgressors your way</u>
- <u>Sinners will turn back to you</u>
- <u>My tongue will sing of your righteousness</u>
- <u>My mouth will declare your praise</u>

Week 5
Lesson 10
96

Jesus' Story Begins— Prophecies and Birth

Stepping Stones

- ➢ Key Figure: Jesus
- ➢ Key Word: Prophecy
- ➢ Key Concept: Jesus fulfills prophecy and is the long-awaited Messiah.
- ➢ Key Scriptures: Luke 1; Matthew 1; Luke 2; Matthew 2

- ➢ **Fulfillment of birth prophecies from the Old Testament**
  - Luke 1:26–38 . . . . Angel's announcement to Mary
  - Matthew 1:1–17 . . . . Genealogy of Jesus
  - Matthew 1:18–25 . . Angel's announcement to Joseph
  - Luke 2:1–7 . . . . Jesus is born
  - Luke 2:8–20 . . . . Angel's announcement to shepherds
  - Luke 2:21–38 . . . . Presentation at the Temple; fulfilling the Law
  - Matthew 2:1–12 . . . . Visit of the Wise Men
  - Matthew 2:13–15 . . Flight to Egypt
  - Matthew 2:16–17 . . Slaughter of the male children in Bethlehem
  - Matthew 2:19–23 . . Return to Nazareth

Materials Needed: Find lesson handouts for participants, available online. Have ready for each student—Christmas gospel tracts and, possibly, small Christmas gifts with a spiritual message. (optional)

Optional: You could consider using clips from *The Jesus Film* to illustrate or introduce episodes from the life of Jesus.

OVERVIEW
Lesson Objectives
- To see that God fulfilled all the prophecies of the Messiah in Jesus Christ.
- To realize that Jesus is the One that was sent by God.

Step 1   Begin the Lesson
- Pray—be sure to begin every lesson with prayer.
- Today we will begin the story of Jesus' wonderful life.
- We will look at prophecies of His birth and how actual events fulfilled them.

Step 2   Review Lessons Up to This Point

- God created a perfect world and placed man in a beautiful garden.
- Man fell into sin, but God offered a remedy immediately. Genesis 3:15
- God chose a man through whom He would bless the whole world—Abraham.
- He made many promises to Abraham:
  - Bless you to be a blessing
  - Bless those who bless you; curse those who curse you
  - Bless all the families of the earth through you
  - Descendants as numerous as the stars and the sand
- God began fulfilling His promises through Abraham and his descendants.
- God saved His people, the Israelites, as well as other nations, through Joseph.
- After 430 years in Egypt, God rescued His people from Egypt through Moses.
- He gave them the Law, the Tabernacle, and Passover to foreshadow Jesus' life and His death on the Cross.
- Later in Israel's history, they asked for a king. Their greatest king was a man after God's own heart, David.
- But even the man after God's own heart sinned. God confronted him, he confessed and God forgave him.
- God promised David that He would establish David's house forever.

Step 3   Jesus Fulfills Prophecy

- Time has passed. It is now the "fullness of time" (Galatians 4:4, "time had fully come") and God is about to act once again to fulfill promises He has made to generations of Abraham's descendants.
- According to scholars, there are over 300 prophecies of Jesus in the Old Testament.
  - It would be highly unlikely for anyone to fulfill all of them if they were not true and if God was not watching over His Word to fulfill it. Jeremiah 1:12
  - Some fulfillments are out of a man's control, such as parentage and birthplace and date of Jesus' birth.
  - Read: "The Coincidence Argument" in *The Case for Christ* by Lee Strobel.
    - Strobel is interviewing Louis S. Lapides, MDiv, ThM, about evidence for Christ:

"First I asked Lapides whether it's possible that Jesus merely fulfilled the prophecies by accident. Maybe He's just one of many throughout history who have coincidentally fit the prophetic fingerprint.

"'Not a chance,' came his response. 'The odds are so astronomical that they rule that out. Someone did the math and

figured out that the probability of just eight prophecies being fulfilled is one chance in one hundred million billion. That number is millions of times greater than the total number of people who've ever walked the planet!

"He calculated that if you took this number of silver dollars, they would cover the state of Texas to a depth of two feet. If you marked one silver dollar among them and then had a blindfolded person wander the whole state and bend down to pick up one coin, what would be the odds he'd choose the one that had been marked?'

"With that he answered his own question: 'The same odds that anybody in history could have fulfilled just eight of the prophecies.'

"I had studied this same statistical analysis by mathematician Peter W. Stoner when I was investigating the messianic prophecies for myself. Stoner also computed that the probability of fulfilling forty-eight prophecies was one chance in a trillion, trillion, trillion, trillion, trillion, trillion, trillion, trillion, trillion, trillion, trillion, trillion, trillion!

"Our minds can't comprehend a number that big. This is a staggering statistic that's equal to the number of minuscule atoms in a trillion, trillion, trillion, trillion, billion universes the size of our universe!

"'The odds alone say it would be impossible for anyone to fulfill the Old Testament prophecies,' Lapides concluded. 'Yet Jesus— and only Jesus throughout all of history—managed to do it.'

"The words of the Apostle Peter popped into my head: 'But the things which God announced beforehand by the mouth of all the prophets, that His Christ should suffer, He has thus fulfilled' (Acts 3:18 NASB)."

- At the end of His earthly life Jesus told His disciples, "This is what I told you while I was still with you: Everything must be fulfilled that is written about me in the Law of Moses, the Prophets and the Psalms." Luke 24:44
- Some prophecies of His birth (Old Testament) and their New Testament fulfillments:

Old Testament	New Testament
Genesis 3:15	Galatians 4:4
Genesis 17:19	Luke 3:34
Numbers 24:17	Matthew 1:2
Genesis 49:10	Luke 3:33
Isaiah 9:7	Luke 1:32–33

Micah 5:2	Luke 2:4–5, 7
Isaiah 7:14	Luke 1:26–27, 30–31
Jeremiah 31:15	Matthew 2:16–18
Hosea 11:1	Matthew 2:14–15

STUDENT GROUP WORK

The student handout for this lesson has some of the prophecies from the Old Testament of Jesus' birth in the left column and the fulfillment references from the New Testament in the right column (see list just provided.)

- Have the students work in pairs. One student could look up the Old Testament verses and the other could look up the New Testament verses.
- Have them make brief notes on what they find. In the handout, one is done as an example.
- Come together as a large group to discuss what they learned. You may want to give them copies of the key to verify accuracy.

Step 4   **Read the Christmas Story**

- Read the Christmas story together. Let different ones read either the full story or focal verses as time allows. Stop periodically and between stories for explanation and questions as needed.
  - Full Christmas story: Luke 1; Matthew 1; Luke 2; Matthew 2
  - Focal verses
    - Luke 1:26–38   Angel's announcement to Mary
    - Matthew 1:1–17   Genealogy of Jesus (the "begats")
      - O Don't skip the "begats." You can learn a lot from them.
      - O For instance, notice which of the Bible characters that you have studied so far are in this list. (Abraham; Judah and his brothers, including Joseph; David)
      - O Also, you may know details about some of the other names you would like to share. For instance, Rahab was a non-Jew and a prostitute. Ruth was a non-Jew and David's great-grandmother. Joseph, Jesus' stepfather, is listed as the husband of Mary, but not the father of Jesus.
    - Matthew 1:18–25   Angel's announcement to Joseph
    - Luke 2:1–7   Jesus is born
    - Luke 2:8–20   Angel's announcement to shepherds
    - Luke 2:21–38   Presentation at the Temple; fulfilling the Law
    - Matthew 2:1–12   Visit of the Wise Men
    - Matthew 2:13–15   Flight to Egypt
    - Matthew 2:16–17   Slaughter of the male children in Bethlehem
    - Matthew 2:19–23   Return to Nazareth

- Or play a Christmas video, such as *The Nativity Story*, or the Christmas portion from *The Jesus Film*, or the beginning of *Magdalena: Through Her Eyes* through the Christmas story.
- Or just read Luke 2, as some families do on Christmas Eve.

★ **Application to Life**

Encourage the students to read the Christmas story (Luke 2) with their families at Christmas.

Step 5 Summary
- Christmas is more than just tinsel and presents.
- Throughout the Old Testament, God was giving many prophecies of a Messiah (Anointed One) that He would send to save the people from their sins.
- All these prophecies were fulfilled in only one man, Jesus Christ.
- He is a historical figure who was born in a real place and really lived on earth.

Step 6 Next Steps
- Possibly give them some small Christmas gift at the end of the lesson. (Example: We have found Christmas cards with Christmas music CDs included for a very low price.)
- Also give them Christmas tracts — a gospel message with a Christmas theme.
- Pray.

HANDOUT KEY: LESSON 11—JESUS' STORY BEGINS— PROPHECIES AND BIRTH

PROPHECY	FULFILLMENT	HOW FULFILLED
Genesis 3:15 Seed of a woman	Galatians 4:4 Born of a woman	Jesus was born of a virgin, i.e. no human father.
Genesis 12:3 Descendent of Abraham	Matthew 1:1 Genealogy of Jesus, "son of Abraham"	God fulfills His promise to bless the whole world through Abraham.
Genesis 17:19 Descendent of Isaac, not Ishmael	Luke 3:34 Genealogy of Jesus, "son of Isaac"	God fulfills His promise to establish His covenant through Isaac.

PROPHECY	FULFILLMENT	HOW FULFILLED
Numbers 24:17 Descendent of Jacob	Matthew 1:2 Genealogy of Jesus, "son of Jacob"	God fulfills His promise of a deliverer through Jacob.
Genesis 49:10 From the tribe of Judah	Luke 3:33 Genealogy of Jesus, "son of Judah"	On his deathbed, Jacob predicted that the scepter would not depart from the tribe of Judah. Jesus is a descendent of this tribe and will reign forever.
Isaiah 9:7 Heir to the throne of David	Luke 1:32–33 Angel tells Mary Jesus will have throne of David	God had made a promise to David to establish his house forever (2 Samuel 7:12–16). The angel tells Mary that God will give her son, Jesus, the throne of David, his ancestor, and that His kingdom will have no end.
Micah 5:2 Born in Bethlehem	Luke 2:4–5, 7 Joseph and Mary travel to Bethlehem; Jesus is born	The prophet Micah identifies a village in Israel that will be the birthplace of the Messiah. A Roman emperor decreed a census (Luke 2:1) that required Joseph and Mary to return to their ancestral home, Bethlehem, David's hometown. While they were there, Jesus was born.
Isaiah 7:14 Born of a virgin	Luke 1:26–27, 34–35 Mary is a virgin	Mary is a virgin when the angel tells her she will have a baby. She asks, "How can this be?" He tells her that the Holy Spirit will overshadow her and her offspring will be called the Son of God.
Jeremiah 31:15 Slaughter of children	Matthew 2:16–18 Herod orders the death of boys up to two years old	Herod was the ruler over Judea and was very paranoid about rivals to his throne. When the magi do not return to tell him where the new king was born, he orders the slaughter of all male children two years old and under in Bethlehem and its surrounding area.
Hosea 11:1 God will call His son from Egypt	Matthew 2:14–15 Mary and Joseph take Jesus to Egypt away from Herod	The prophecy in Hosea is both a recounting of the Exodus and a prophecy for the Messiah. When Herod ordered the slaughter in Bethlehem, an angel warned Joseph to take the child to Egypt. The Gospel writer saw this as a fulfillment of this prophecy in Hosea.

Source: The Open Bible

Jesus—Introduction and Teachings

Stepping Stones
> ➢ Key Figure: Jesus
> ➢ Key Word: Teaching
> ➢ Key Concept: Jesus begins His ministry and begins teaching the people.
> ➢ Key Scripture: John 1–3

Preparation: Highlight the verses in the lesson that you will reference during the lesson. You may want to write these references on the board so the students will have them when you mention them during the lesson. Find lesson handouts for participants, as well as a list of verses not referenced on their handouts, available online.

103

OVERVIEW
Lesson Objectives
- To see how Jesus began His ministry.
- To begin to learn something of His character from the things He does.

Step 1   Begin the Lesson
- Pray—be sure to begin every lesson with prayer.
- Today we will see how Jesus began His teaching ministry.

Step 2   Review
- God has been progressively revealing how He would use Abraham's descendants to bless the world. God ultimately and completely fulfilled those promises by sending Jesus.
- In the last lesson, we saw how Jesus was born and noted that He fulfilled Old Testament prophecies of the Messiah.
- Now we will begin looking at who He was and what He did.

Step 3   Introducing Jesus—John 1:29–34
- After Herod died, Jesus and his family left Egypt and went back to Nazareth.
  - There Jesus spent a **quiet** childhood. Luke 2:51–52

- "And Jesus grew in wisdom and stature, and in favor with God and men."
- When He was 30 years old, it was time to begin His public ministry.
- <u>John</u> the <u>Baptist</u> was sent by God to be the forerunner of Jesus, to announce His arrival, as predicted in Isaiah (John 1:23), but he was very clear to say that he was not the <u>Messiah</u> (John 1:20, 26–27).
  - Note: Messiah and Christ are both terms for the promised anointed one. Messiah is Hebrew, Christ is Greek.
- Read John 1:29–34.
- Jesus came to John the Baptist for <u>baptism</u>.
  - Here John the Baptist answers <u>Isaac's</u> question, "Where is the <u>Lamb</u>?" Genesis 22:7–8
  - When <u>John</u> saw Jesus approaching, he said, "Behold the <u>Lamb</u>." John 1:29
- Jesus' baptism was accompanied by miraculous signs.
  - "I saw the <u>Spirit</u> come down from heaven as a <u>dove</u> and remain on him." John 1:32
- God told John the Baptist that these signs point to the One, and John testified that this is the Son of God. John 1:33–34

Step 4   Jesus Begins His ministry: Cleansing the Temple—John 2:12–25

- Read John 2:12–17.
- Early in Jesus' ministry we see what is important to Him. He visits the Temple and finds the merchants buying and selling in the Temple. He clears them out.
- Draw a plan of the Temple on the board or a flip pad. (The Outer Court of Herod's Temple) See drawing provided.
  - Include the following:
    - Temple — Holy place and Most Holy place
    - Court of the Priests
    - Court of Israel (Men)
    - Court of the Women
    - Court of the Gentiles

★ Explain

Explain that each group could only go as far as their group was allowed. So the men could go through the outside two courts to get to their area, but were not allowed to go into the Court of the Priests. The women could pass through the Court of the Gentiles, but could not go into the Court of the Men. And the Gentiles were not allowed past the Court of the Gentiles.

THE TEMPLE COMPLEX

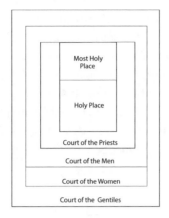

```
Most Holy
Place

Holy Place

Court of the Priests

Court of the Men

Court of the Women

Court of the Gentiles
```

- The merchants were in the Court of the Gentiles. Why did this make Jesus angry?
  - What was one of the major purposes God had in calling Abraham?
    - To bless the nations, the Gentiles, through him Genesis 12:3b; Galatians 3:8

  - The merchants were actually performing an important service: **selling** sacrificial animals and **exchanging** foreign currency for temple money for worshippers who had traveled to Jerusalem for the feast as required by the Law. (The Cleansing of the Temple) Deuteronomy 14:22–27
  - But the merchants were disturbing the **Gentiles** as they worshipped in the only part of the temple area where they were allowed (The Outer Court of Herod's Temple): the Court of the Gentiles.

★ Application to Life

Do we sometimes make it hard for people to worship? What are some ways we do this?
- Not inviting our family, friends, and neighbors to join us for worship.
- Talking loudly in church before the service, keeping people from preparing themselves for worship.
- Talking only to people we know and not welcoming visitors.
- Gossiping about others in church.
- Talking about other things rather than focusing on God and what we are about to do in worship.

  - Jesus quotes two Old Testament prophets — Isaiah 56:6–7 and Jeremiah 7:11.

- See also: Matthew 21:13; Mark 11:17; Luke 19:46.
- The prophets and Jesus also say the merchants were making the Temple a robber's den, so they were probably cheating the people.
- The Temple was to be the **House** of **Prayer**. The merchants were keeping the **nations**, the Gentiles, from worshipping God. And they were **robbing** people in God's house. These two actions defame God before the people that God was trying to bless through Abraham's descendants.
- The apostles remembered Psalm 69:9: "Zeal for your house will consume me."
- Jesus' anger is **righteous** anger. He is defending the Temple, God's name, and the purpose of the promise made to Abraham—to bless all nations through his descendants.

★ Teacher's Note

John records this event at the beginning of Jesus' ministry, but Matthew, Mark, and Luke record a similar event in Jesus' last week on earth, before the Cross. (Matthew 21:12–13; Mark 11:15–18; Luke 19:28–48) This incident later in His ministry further stirred the Jewish leaders to destroy Jesus.

Week 6
Lesson 12
106

★ Application to Life

The Bible does not say all anger is a sin.
- There are many places in Scripture that describe God as being angry, usually at sin in His people, such as in Deuteronomy 9:7; 13:17.
- God is slow to anger and He is merciful. Psalm 103:8–10
- Psalm 30:5 "For his anger lasts only a moment, but his favor lasts a lifetime; weeping may remain for a night, but rejoicing comes in the morning."

Have students read Ephesians 4:26–27.
- "'In your anger do not sin' (quote of Psalm 4:4): Do not let the sun go down while you are still angry, and do not give the devil a foothold."
- Anger that is **mishandled** becomes sin and gives the devil **a way to get to us**.

The Bible does have admonitions concerning anger.
- Have the students look at the "Some Bible Verses about Anger" handout (available online).
- They can also look up additional references using a concordance.
- Show a concordance and tell how to use it.

Step 5   Jesus Teaches a Teacher — John 3:1–21
- Read John 3:1–21.

- Who is Nicodemus? A **Pharisee** and a member of the Jewish ruling council (Sanhedrin)
  - Define Pharisee.
    - The name means "separated ones."
    - A Jewish sect
    - Knowledgeable of the Scriptures
    - Very careful to follow Moses's Law, but focused more on outward details rather than the heart Matthew 23:23
    - They clashed often with Jesus. They were one of the only groups Jesus criticized publicly: religious leaders.
    - Not all of them were bad. Some were truly seeking, but they were in the minority.
  - Define Jewish ruling council.
    - Called the Sanhedrin
    - Presided over by the high priest
    - Had religious and civil authority but was subordinate to the Romans in civil law during the Roman occupation
- Look at what Nicodemus says and how Jesus responds. John 3:2–3

  - Nicodemus identifies Jesus as a **teacher** and a **miracle worker**.
  - Jesus does not waste time. He cuts to the heart of what Nicodemus needs to hear.
  - He then clarifies who He is and why He came.
- Jesus says we must be **born again** to see the **kingdom** of God.
  - We hear the phrase "born again" a lot in our culture.
  - Nicodemus is the first to hear it and he is confused. What is he thinking of? **Physical birth** (John 3:4)
- So Jesus explains. John 3:5–8
  - There are two **births**: a **physical** birth and a **spiritual** birth.
  - He also says that, just like the wind, you can see the effects of the spiritual birth, but you can't see where it is coming from or where it is going.
    - The spiritual birth is not something you can see from the outside, but you see its effects.
    - In Matthew 7:15–20 (especially verse 20) Jesus shows one of the effects you can see: "Thus by their fruit you will recognize them."
- Nicodemus is still confused. John 3:9
- Jesus says Nicodemus is the teacher of Israel and rebukes him for not understanding. If Nicodemus doesn't understand this, how will he understand other things? John 3:10–12
- In John 3:13 Jesus calls Himself the Son of Man. Who is the Son of Man?
  - This was Jesus' favorite term for Himself. It shows Him as both man and God.

- It was a reference to the Messiah. Daniel 7:13–14
- Jesus says He is the only one who has been to heaven. John 3:13
- In verse 14, He says He must be lifted up as Moses lifted up the snake in the desert.
  - This is a reference to Numbers 21:4–9.
  - The people of Israel had spoken against Moses and against God, so God sent venomous snakes into the camp.
  - The people realized their sin and asked for the snakes to be removed.
  - God told Moses to put a snake on a pole. Anyone who looked at it would be saved.
  - This foreshadows the Cross. Jesus became sin (2 Corinthians 5:21) on the Cross. When we believe in Him (look on the Cross), we are saved from sin (have eternal life).
- John 3:16 is one of the best loved and most recognized verses in the Bible. It is the gospel in a nutshell.

★ Discover John 3:16 Together

Have the students look at each phrase of John 3:16. Have them tell what they think each phrase means. Below are suggested answers.

For God	*the Initiator*
So loved	*why He did what He did*
The world	*who benefited; includes everyone*
That he gave	*what He did; sacrifice, gift*
His one and only son	*what He gave*
That whoever	*who can benefit; whoever responds in faith*
Believes in Him	*what we must do*
Shall not perish	*what doesn't happen to us: mercy*
But have eternal life	*what we gain: grace*

- Jesus' purpose — John 3:17–18
  - Why did Jesus come into the world? Not to **condemn**, but to **save**

★ Application to Life

Be careful not to miss the grace and mercy of God.
Yes, we do sin.
Yes, there are consequences. (Remember David's story?)
But, there is also mercy, grace, and forgiveness.
Mercy: **not getting what we deserve**
Grace: **getting what we don't deserve**

- Who is saved from condemnation? The one who **believes** in Him. John 3:18
- Jesus does not condemn the rest. They stand condemned because they **don't believe**. John 3:18

Step 6   Summary
- John the Baptist had been preparing the people for the arrival of the Messiah.
- John recognized Him by the signs from God.
- Jesus got right to the business of showing people who He was and what He had come to do: to glorify God and to save people from their sins.

Step 7   Next Steps
- Next lesson, we will learn more about Jesus as we see Him performing miracles and healing people.
- Pray.

HANDOUT KEY: LESSON 12—
JESUS—INTRODUCTION AND TEACHINGS

Introducing Jesus — John 1:29–34
- Jesus had a **quiet** childhood. Luke 2:51–52
- **John** the **Baptist** was the forerunner of Jesus. John 1:23
- He made sure people knew that he was not the **Messiah**. John 1:20, 26–27
- Jesus comes to him for **baptism**.

Jesus comes toward him and the people, and John the Baptist answers an important question.
- **Isaac** asked, "Where is the **Lamb**?" Genesis 22:7–8
- **John the Baptist** said, "Behold the **Lamb**." John 1:29

John saw the miraculous sign of the **Spirit** of God coming down on Him like a **dove**. John 1:32

Cleansing the Temple — John 2:12–25
- Draw a plan of the temple courts.
- Why were the merchants in the Temple?
  - **Selling** sacrificial animals and **exchanging** money
- The merchants were keeping the **Gentiles** from God.
- This presented problems. Jesus quotes two Old Testament prophets: Isaiah 56:6–7 and Jeremiah 7:11, and the apostles remembered Psalm 69:9. (See also Matthew 21:13; Mark 11:17; Luke 19:46.) **What do we learn from these verses?**

- The Temple was to be the **House** of **Prayer** for all **nations.**
- They were **robbing** the people in God's house.

- Jesus' anger is **righteous** anger. He is defending the Temple, God's name, and the purpose of the promise made to Abraham—to bless all nations through his descendants. It is the shepherd's job to protect the flock, and that is what Jesus is doing here.
- Ephesians 4:26–27: Anger that is **mishandled** becomes sin and gives the devil **a way to get to us.**

Jesus Teaches a Teacher—John 3:1–21

- Who is Nicodemus? A **Pharisee**
- Nicodemus identifies Jesus as a **teacher** and a **miracle worker.**
- Jesus says we must be **born again** to see the **kingdom** of God.
- What does Nicodemus think Jesus is talking about? **Physical birth**
- Jesus explains that there are two **births**: **physical** and **spiritual**

Look at each phrase of John 3:16, the gospel (good news) in a nutshell.

- For God   <u>the Initiator</u>
- So loved   <u>why He did what He did</u>
- The world   <u>who benefited; includes everyone</u>
- That he gave   <u>what He did; sacrifice, gift</u>
- His one and only son   <u>what He gave</u>
- That whoever   <u>who can benefit; whoever responds in faith</u>
- Believes in Him   <u>what we must do</u>
- Shall not perish   <u>what doesn't happen to us: mercy</u>
- But have eternal life   <u>what we gain: grace</u>

Why did Jesus come into the world? Not to **condemn**, but to **save.**

- Who is saved from condemnation? The one who **believes** in Him.
- Definition of *mercy*: **not getting what we deserve**
- Definition of *grace*: **getting what we don't deserve**
- Jesus does not condemn the rest. They stand condemned because they **don't believe.**

 # Jesus—Miracles

Stepping Stones

> ➢ Key Figure: Jesus
> ➢ Key Word: Believe
> ➢ Key Concept: Jesus' miracles show who He is so that we may believe.
> ➢ Key Scriptures: Passages in the four Gospels

Note: The Optional Lesson on John 9—The Man Born Blind can be taught in lieu of this lesson. Find lesson handouts for participants, available online.

OVERVIEW

Lesson Objectives

- To see why Jesus performed miracles.
- To see what His miracles teach us.
- To see how people reacted to miracles.

Step 1 Definition

- Pray — be sure to begin every lesson with prayer.
- Ask the question: What do you consider to be a miracle?
- What is a miracle?
  - "an effect or extraordinary event in the physical world that surpasses all known human or natural powers and is ascribed to a supernatural cause." (Dictionary.com)
- Ask the class about any miracles in their lives or the lives of those around them.

Step 2 Jesus Begins His Ministry

- Read Luke 4:14–21.
- At the beginning of His ministry, after he had fasted 40 days in the wilderness, Jesus came to Nazareth, His hometown, and went to the synagogue on the Sabbath.
- At the synagogue that day, Jesus was asked to read from Isaiah. He read a passage (61:1–2a) that spoke of the Messiah, the One who was to come from God, for whom the Jews had been waiting hundreds of years.

111

- What happened after He read this passage?
  - He sat down and all the people looked at Him.
  - Then He said the Scripture had been fulfilled just then.
- What was He saying to them? He is the Messiah.
- According to the passage in Isaiah, what kinds of things would the Messiah do?
  - Preach good news to the poor
  - Proclaim freedom for the prisoners
  - Restore sight to the blind
  - Release the oppressed
  - Proclaim the year of the Lord's favor

★ Teacher's Note

The year of the Lord's favor is the Jubilee year. It was supposed to happen every 50 years and was to be a new start for all. Leviticus 25:10

- Have the students summarize what these verses say about the work of the Messiah.
  - **He would preach.**
  - **He would do miracles.**
  - **He would bring freedom and a new start.**
- Jesus used this verse to characterize His ministry. The Book of Luke goes on to show how Jesus fulfilled these verses that He had read from Isaiah.

Step 3   What Do the Miracles of Jesus Teach Us?
- Jesus' miracles show that He is the **Messiah**, the One Sent by God.
  - Jesus fulfilled **prophecy**.
    - We just saw that Jesus said the verses in Isaiah 61 were **fulfilled** in Him.
    - Read Matthew 8:16–17.
    - In this chapter, Jesus had spent a long day healing the people.
      - ○ A man with leprosy Matthew 8:2–4
      - ○ A centurion's servant Matthew 8:5–13
      - ○ Peter's mother-in-law Matthew 8:14–15
      - ○ Many sick and demon-possessed Matthew 8:16
    - What reason does Matthew give us for all these miracles? "This was to **fulfill** what was spoken through the prophet Isaiah." Matthew then goes on to quote Isaiah 53:4.
  - When Jesus performed miracles, the people realized that there was something special about Him.
    - Luke 7:16 Jesus raised the son of a widow of Nain.

- ○ They were **filled with awe** and **praised God**.
- ○ They said, "A great prophet has appeared among us. **God** has come to help His people."
  - John 7:31 The Jewish leaders had tried to seize Jesus, but many in the crowd said, "When the **Christ** comes, will he do more miraculous **signs** than this man?"
- Jesus' miracles teach us about **God and His ways**.
  - His miracles reveal His and God's **glory**.
    - Read John 2:11.
      - ○ At the beginning of His ministry, John records that Jesus turned water into wine at a wedding feast.
      - ○ John called it "the first of his miraculous signs."
      - ○ John also said that "He thus revealed his **glory**."
    - Read John 9:3.
      - ○ When Jesus and His disciples passed by a man born blind, the disciples asked who sinned.
      - ○ Jesus answered that it was not caused by sin, "but this happened so that the **work** of God might be **displayed** in his life."
    - Read John 11:4.
      - ○ Jesus gets news that his friend, Lazarus, is sick.
      - ○ What does Jesus say is the reason for this sickness? "This **sickness** will not end in **death**. No, it is for **God's** glory so that God's **Son** may be glorified through it."
  - Jesus' miracles explain the truth about **sickness**.
    - We already saw in John 9:3 (man born blind) and 11:4 (raising of Lazarus) that Jesus had a different perspective on sickness and death.
    - The people of that time believed that bad things happened to bad people. But here were two instances where the bad thing was not caused by sin. Instead it was what God used to reveal His and His Son's glory.
    - Sickness entered the world because of sin. It is a condition of our fallen world. However, a person's sickness is not always caused because they, or someone close to them, sinned.
    - God does not cause sickness, but sometimes He uses it to show His glory.
  - His miracles teach a proper understanding of the **Sabbath**.
    - In several incidents, Jesus heals a person on the Sabbath, often in the synagogue (place of worship).
    - The Jews had many rules about the Sabbath, God's weekly day of rest and worship, and had gone far beyond God's original intent for the day.

- The Sabbath was on the last day of the week, Saturday, and was a holy day of rest set aside by God. Genesis 2:3
- There are many things said in the Law of Moses about how the Jews were to treat the Sabbath.
- In the years before Jesus came, the Jewish leaders had added even more restrictions to the Sabbath.
- The Jewish leaders were looking for a way to accuse Jesus because they thought He was a threat.
- They often attacked Him when He healed on the Sabbath, accusing Him of violating the Law by working on the day of rest.
  - The Jewish leaders saw healing as **work.**
  - Jesus saw healing as **compassion, care.**
- Over and over again, Jesus turned the focus back on **God** and on **people,** by ignoring man-made rules and fulfilling the real meaning of the Sabbath.
  - A man with a shriveled hand. Mark 3:1–6
    Mark 3:4 "Which is lawful on the Sabbath: to do good or to do evil, to save life or to kill?"

  - A bent-over woman who was crippled by a spirit for 18 years. Luke 13:10–17
    Luke 13:16 "Then should not this woman, a daughter of Abraham, whom Satan has kept bound for eighteen long years, be set free on the Sabbath day from what bound her?" He contrasted this to the Jews who would take care of an *animal* on the Sabbath, but didn't want Him to help the *woman* on the Sabbath.
  - A man suffering from dropsy. Luke 14:1–6
    Luke 14:3 "Is it lawful to heal on the Sabbath or not?" Here again, He contrasted their treatment of their animals with that of the man who stood before them.
  - A man who had been paralyzed for 38 years. John 5:1–15
    John 5:17 "My Father is always at his work to this very day, and I too, am working." He is doing the Father's work.
- Jesus' miracles show us **His heart.**
  - Jesus has compassion on people.
    - Read Luke 7:12–13. What was the miracle in this passage? **Jesus raised the son of the widow of Nain.**
    - What reason is given for this miracle? **Compassion: His heart went out to her.**
    - For more examples, see these passages.
      - Matthew 15:32–39 **fed the four thousand**
      - Matthew 20:29–34 **healed two blind men**

- Jesus rewards **faith**
  - Read Matthew 9:20–22 Once there was a woman who had been subject to bleeding for 12 years.
  - She bravely reached out to touch Jesus' cloak, believing that if she did, she would be healed.
  - What did Jesus tell her when He realized what she had done? "Your faith has healed you." And she was healed from that moment. Matthew 9:22
  - This is only one of many times that Jesus told people that their faith had healed them.

★ Teacher's Note

Be sensitive here. Sometimes God does not heal even when we have believed.

Let God be God. He is still in control even if He does not give the miracle that we have prayed for.

Daniel's three friends said that God was able to protect them but, even if He didn't, they would not bow down to the king's statue. Daniel 3:16–18

Even Jesus did not heal everyone He encountered.
- *In Mark 1:29–39, Jesus had been healing many sick and demon-possessed. Now many people were coming to Him. Early in the morning, Jesus took a break and went to pray. His disciples found Him and said everyone was looking for Him. Jesus said they needed to go to other towns for Him to preach even though there was a crowd waiting for healing.*
- *In John 5:1–15, Jesus healed a man who had been waiting by the pool for 38 years. But there were other sick people waiting for a healing and Jesus did not heal them.*

- Jesus has authority to **forgive sin.**
  - Read Matthew 9:1–8.
  - What was wrong with the man who was brought before Jesus? He was **paralyzed**.
  - What did Jesus do first for the paralytic? **Forgave his sins**
  - Jesus knew the leaders were thinking that He had blasphemed (sinned).
  - What did He do in order to prove to them that He had the authority to forgive sin (where they could not see the effects)? He **healed** the man (where they could see the results).

Step 4   Why Did Jesus Perform Miracles?
- **Jesus' miracles testify of Him.**
  - Read John 3:2. Nicodemus, a ruler of the Jews, said that Jesus could not do the miracles He did unless **God was with Him.**

- Read John 5:36. Jesus' work **testifies** that the Father sent Him.
- Read Acts 2:22. Even in the Book of Acts, after Jesus had returned to the Father, Peter reminded the people that God used Jesus' **miracles** to prove to them **who Jesus was**.
- Jesus' miracles are given as signs to help us believe.
  - Read John 20:30–31.
  - John only recorded a few of Jesus' miracles, which he called "signs."
  - What does John say could happen if we read even the few signs he had recorded.
    - **We can believe that Jesus is the Christ (Messiah).**
    - **We can know that He is the Son of God.**
    - **By believing, we will have eternal life.**

★ Teacher's Note

There are several places in the Book of John where Jesus speaks of His works and our belief.

- *In John 10, during a discussion that Jesus had with the Jewish leaders, they asked Him to tell them plainly if He was the Christ. He answered, "I did tell you, but you do not believe. The miracles I do in my Father's name speak for me" (John 10:25).*
- *Later in that same discussion, Jesus said, "Do not believe me unless I do what my Father does. But if I do it, even though you do not believe me, believe the miracles, that you may know and understand that the Father is in me, and I in the Father" (John 10:37–38).*
- *In the upper room after the Last Supper, Jesus told the disciples to "Believe me when I say that I am in the Father and the Father is in me; or at least believe on the evidence of the miracles themselves" (John 14:11).*
- *Jesus would prefer that we **believe Him** based on His **Word** alone. But if we can't, then we should start with the **miracles**.*

Step 5 How Did People React to the Miracles?

★ Encourage students to put themselves at the scene

Imagine that you lived in first-century Israel. You have heard about a man who has been healing people and performing many miracles. Then one day He comes to your town and heals a friend of yours from a disease that everyone thought would take her life. How would you react?

- Many times in the Gospels, we read that the people were **amazed** and the **news** about Jesus **spread,** as in Mark 1:27–28; Luke 7:16–17.
- Often after a miracle, many people would **put their faith in Jesus**. For instance, after Jesus raised his friend, Lazarus, from the dead it says, "Therefore many of the Jews who had come to visit Mary, and had seen what Jesus did, put their faith in him" (John 11:45).
  - Note: Mary was one of Lazarus's sisters who was grieving his death.
- However, not everyone reacted **positively.**
  - The next verse says, "But some of them went to the Pharisees and told them what Jesus had done" (John 11:46).
  - After this, the Pharisees plotted how they might kill Jesus (John 11:53) and later plotted to kill Lazarus, too (John 12:10–11), because people were believing in Jesus after He had raised Lazarus.
- This shows that miracles can help people believe, but not always. Miracles don't necessarily produce faith. Some people **believe** after seeing a miracle, but some **don't**.
- Jesus knew that not everyone who saw a miracle would believe in Him, but He held unbelievers **accountable.**

  - "Then Jesus began to denounce the cities in which most of his miracles had been performed, because they did not repent" (Matthew 11:20).
  - "If I had not done among them what no one else did, they would not be guilty of sin. But now they have seen these miracles, and yet they have hated both me and my Father. But this is to fulfill what is written in their Law: 'They hated me without reason'" (John 15:24–25).

Step 6   Summary
- Jesus came as a "man accredited by God to you by miracles, wonders and signs" (Acts 2:22).
- His miracles fulfilled prophecy, showing that He was the One promised and sent by God.
- Jesus used miracles to teach us about Himself and His Father, about sickness and the Sabbath, about what it means to believe and about forgiveness.
- These were also signs that we may believe in Him and have life in His name. (See John 20:31.)

Step 7   Next Steps
- In the next lesson, we will look at how Jesus identifies Himself with God in the Book of John.
- Pray.

Jesus Began His Ministry. Luke 4:14–21.

What do the verses Jesus read say about the work of the Messiah?

- <u>He would preach</u>.
- <u>He would do miracles</u>.
- <u>He would bring freedom and a new start</u>.

What do the miracles of Jesus teach us?

Jesus' miracles show that He is the <u>Messiah</u>, the One sent by God.

- Jesus fulfilled <u>prophecy</u>.
  - Jesus said the verses in Isaiah 61 were <u>fulfilled</u> in Him.
  - What reason does Matthew give us for all the miracles? Matthew 8:17
    - "This was to <u>fulfill</u> what was spoken through the prophet Isaiah." Isaiah 53:4

- When Jesus performed miracles, the people realized that there was something special about Him.
  - When Jesus raised the son of a widow, how did the people react? Luke 7:16
    - They were <u>filled with awe</u> and <u>praised God</u>.
    - They said, "<u>God</u> has come to help His people."
  - When the Jewish leaders tried to seize Jesus, what question did the people in the crowd ask? John 7:31
    - "When the <u>Christ</u> comes, will he do more miraculous <u>signs</u> than this man?"

Jesus' miracles teach us about <u>God and His ways</u>.

- His miracles reveal His and God's <u>glory</u>.
  - John 2:11
    - Turning water into wine was "the first of his miraculous signs."
    - Here, "He thus revealed his <u>glory</u>."
  - John 9:3
    - When the disciples saw a man who had been born blind, they asked who sinned.
    - Jesus answered that it was not caused by sin, "but this happened so that the <u>work</u> of God might be <u>displayed</u> in his life."
  - John 11:4
    - What does Jesus say is the reason for Lazarus' sickness?
    - "This <u>sickness</u> will not end in <u>death</u>. No, it is for <u>God's</u> glory so that God's <u>Son</u> may be glorified through it."

- Jesus' miracles explain the truth about __sickness__.
- His miracles teach a proper understanding of the __Sabbath__.
  - The Jewish leaders say healing as __work__.
  - Jesus saw healing as __compassion/care__.
  - Over and over again, Jesus turned the focus back on __God__ and on __people__.
    - Mark 3:4 _____
      _____
    - Luke 13:16 _____
      _____
    - Luke 14:3 _____
      _____
    - John 5:17 _____
      _____

Jesus' miracles show us __His heart__.
- Jesus is compassionate.
  - What was the miracle in Luke 7:12–13?
    - __Jesus raised the son of the widow of Nain__
  - What reason is given for the miracle in this passage?
    - __Compassion/His heart went out to them__
  - For more examples, see these passages—Matthew 15:32; Matthew 20:29–34
- Jesus rewards __faith__.
- Jesus has authority to __forgive sin__.
  - What was wrong with the man who was brought before Jesus? Matthew 9:1–8.
    - He was __paralyzed__.
  - What did Jesus do first for the paralytic?
    - __Forgave his sins__
  - What did he do in order to prove to them that He had the authority to forgive sin (where they could not see the effects)?
    - He __healed__ the man (where they could see the results).

Why did Jesus perform miracles?
Jesus' miracles testify of Him.
- John 3:2 Nicodemus said that Jesus could not do the miracles He did unless __God was with Him__.
- John 5:36 Jesus' work __testifies__ that the Father sent Him.
- Acts 2:22 Peter reminded the people that God used Jesus' __miracles__ to prove to them __who Jesus was__.

Jesus' miracles are given as signs to help us believe. John 20:31

- What does John say could happen if we read even the few signs he had recorded.
  - **We can believe that Jesus is the Christ (Messiah).**
  - **We can know that He is the Son of God.**
  - **By believing, we may have eternal life.**
- Jesus would prefer that we **believe Him** based on His **Word** alone. But if we can't, then we should start with the **miracles**.

How did people react to the miracles?
People were **amazed** and the **news** about Jesus **spread**. (e.g. Mark 1:27–28, Luke 7:16–17)
Often after a miracle, many people would **put their faith in Jesus**. (e.g. John 11:45)
However, not everyone reacted **positively**. (John 11:46, 53; 12:10–11)
Some people **believe** after seeing a miracle, but some **don't**.
Even so, Jesus held the unbelievers **accountable**. (Matthew 11:20, John 15:24–25)

Nature of Jesus—I AM Statements in the Book of John

Stepping Stones

> ➤ Key Figure: Jesus
> ➤ Key Word: Identity
> ➤ Key Concept: Jesus identifies Himself with the Father.
> ➤ Key Bible Book: John
>
> ➤ **Focal Verses**
> * Before Abraham was born, I am! . . . . . John 8:58
> * Pre-existence of Christ . . . . John 1:1–3; Genesis 1:26
> * I am the Bread of Life . . . . John 6:35, 48–51
> * I am the Light of the World . . . . John 8:12; 9:5
> * I am the Gate of the Sheep . . . . John 10:7, 9
> * I am the Good Shepherd . . . . John 10:11, 14
> * I am the Resurrection and the Life . . . John 11:25
> * I am the Way, Truth, Life . . . . John 14:6
> * I am the True Vine . . . . John 15:1, 5

OVERVIEW
Lesson Objective
* To see how Jesus identifies Himself as God using the name God gave to Moses— I AM.

Step 1   Begin the Lesson
* Pray—be sure to begin every lesson with prayer.
* Today we will see that Jesus is God. Over and over again He uses the name of God that God gave to Moses—I AM—in Exodus 3:14 when Moses asked Him who was sending him.
* We will also see from their reactions that the Jewish leaders understood what Jesus was claiming.

Step 2   Review
* We have been getting to know Jesus.
* We looked at how He was born and how His birth fulfilled prophecies of the Messiah from the Old Testament.

- Next, we saw Jesus as He was introduced by His forerunner, John the Baptist, "Behold the Lamb." John 1:29, 36
- Then we saw Him as He began His ministry, cleansing the temple and teaching a teacher, Nicodemus. There we began to see what was important to Jesus.
- In our last lesson, we talked about Jesus' miracles and healings.
- Now we will look at who He claimed to be. Some say He was a prophet, a teacher, or a great man, and He was those things. But that is not all. He said, and Scripture confirms, that He is God.

Step 3   Introduction
- Today, we will look a little more closely at the nature of Jesus.
- In the Gospel of John there are many "I AM" statements.
- We have heard this phrase before, "I AM"; do you remember what it is?
  - **It is God's name as He revealed it to Moses** (Exodus 3:14).
- John quotes Jesus using this name to show who He is.
- When Jesus makes these "I AM" statements, He is identifying Himself with God in the Old Testament. And as we will see, the Jewish leaders don't miss the point.

- The Israelites were very aware of this name, as they should have been.
  - In Old Testament texts the name was written as **YHWH** with no vowels.
  - It was used more than 6,000 times in the Old Testament texts. In modern English translations it is often written LORD (all capital letters).
  - Out of reverence, the Israelites didn't speak this name, and over time the actual pronunciation was lost. Now it is pronounced: Yah-weh.
  - The Latinized form of the name is Jehovah.

Step 4   Before Abraham Was Born, I Am! John 8:58–59
(Pre-existence of Christ: also John 1:1–3; Genesis 1:26)
- Read John 8:56–59.
- In John, chapters 7 and 8, Jesus is having a long discussion with the Jewish leaders about who He is and who they were. He makes this statement, "I tell you the truth, before Abraham was born, I am!" John 8:58
- What does Jesus communicate with this statement?
  - Jesus uses the name that God gave to Moses.
  - He is saying, "**I am God.**"
  - He states that **He existed before Abraham**.
- John began his Gospel with John 1:1–2 where we see that Jesus has been with God from the beginning and is, in fact, God.
- John 1:3 states that Jesus is the **Creator**. This means He existed before He came in the flesh (was incarnated). (See also Genesis 1:26.)
- The Jewish leaders don't miss the point.

- What do they try to do? Stone Him
- Why? They knew He was saying that He is God because He used God's name.
- Later, when the high priest was interrogating Jesus, he asked, "Are you the Christ, the Son of the Blessed One?" (Mark 14:61–62) Jesus answered, "I am."
  - Jesus then continued with a description of Himself that fit the Messiah, quoting Daniel 7:13–14, a Messianic passage.
  - The high priest tore his clothes and called Jesus' statements blasphemy, then they condemned Him to death. Once again, they did not miss the point of His statement, "I am God."
- Summary: Jesus is **God**.

Step 5   I Am the Bread of Life—John 6:25–35, 48–51

- In John 6, Jesus fed the five thousand then departed from them. Some searched for Him.
- Read John 6:26–27. When they found Him, Jesus rebuked them, saying they had searched for Him because they had eaten and had their fill. Then He told them not to work for food that **spoils**, but for food that **endures** to eternal **life**, that the Son of Man would give them.

- John 6:30–35 They asked for a sign like the manna Moses gave them in the desert. Jesus told them that "the bread of God is he who comes down from heaven and gives life to the world."
  - Read John 6:33–35.
  - When they asked for this bread, Jesus said, "I am the **bread** of **life**."
- John 6:48–66 Jesus repeated that He is the bread of life. He reminded them that their fathers ate manna, but still died. He then said that He is the living bread from heaven, and that if they eat this bread they will never die. Some of them were offended and departed from following Him (John 6:51–58, 60, 66).
- What might they have thought He was saying?
  - Cannibalism?
  - They were thinking of the physical.
- What was He really saying?
  - He points them to the spiritual.
  - Who is the bread of life? Jesus

★ Application to Life

What does it mean to "eat the bread of life"?
- **"Eating the bread" means trusting the sacrifice He made for our sins and gaining eternal life.**
  - John 6:29 To "believe in Him" means to commit ourselves to Him, not just believe what He says (John 6:30).

- John 6:51 The bread is His flesh that He gave for the life of the world. This is a reference to His sacrifice on the Cross.
- John 6:54 Whoever eats His flesh and drinks His blood has eternal life. We gain eternal life through belief in Christ and the sacrifice He made.

- **"Eating the bread" means feeding on the Word**.
  Jeremiah 15:16: "When your words came, I ate them; they were my joy and my heart's delight, for I bear your name, O LORD God Almighty."
  - **Spend time *in* the Word (the Bible).**
    "The Spirit gives life; the flesh counts for nothing. The words I have spoken to you are spirit and they are life." John 6:63
  - **Spend time *with* the Word.**
    Jesus is called the Word. John 1:1
    - Physical bodies need daily physical food. Spiritual bodies need daily spiritual food.
    - *The Holman Bible Dictionary* describes it as "actively coming to Him and drawing life-giving strength from Him."
- **"Eating the bread" means obeying the Father.** John 4:34

- Summary: Jesus and His Word are our **spiritual food.**

Step 6   I Am the Light of the World — John 8:12; 9:5

- Another time Jesus told the Jews, "I am the **light** of the **world**. Whoever follows me will never walk in darkness, but will have the light of life." John 8:12
- Again in John 9:5, He says, "While I am in the world, I am the light of the world."
- When do we need light? When it is **dark**
  - Proverbs 4:19: "But the way of the wicked is like deep darkness, they do not know what makes them stumble."
  - Darkness = sin, judgment, being lost
- We see in John 1:4 that in Him was life, and that life was the light of men.
- In John 1:9, He is called the true light that gives light to every man.
- Other references to light in the Bible:
  - 1 John 1:5: "God is light; in him there is no darkness at all."
  - Psalm 27:1: "The Lord is my light and my salvation — whom shall I fear?"
  - Psalm 119:105: "Your word is a lamp to my feet and a light for my path."
- Once again, what is one way that we experience Him as light? **In His Word**
- Summary: Jesus **shows the way, reveals.**

Step 7   I am the Gate, the Door of the Sheep—John 10:7, 9

- Read John 10:7–10 aloud.
- John 10:7, 9: "I am the **gate** for the **sheep**."

- Draw a sheepfold with a shepherd as the doorway.

- In Jesus' time, the shepherds kept their flocks on open land.
- At night they built a sheepfold with rocks.
- One of the shepherds would sleep in the doorway to keep out predators.
- Function of the gate, door
  - **Access**: It was the only way in. John 10:9
  - **Protection:** The shepherd in the doorway only lets sheep in and out, not predators.
- Summary: Jesus is **the only way** in and is our **protection**.

Step 8   I Am the Good Shepherd—John 10:11, 14

- John 10:11, 14: "I am the **Good Shepherd**."
- Ask the students, "What does a shepherd do for his sheep?" Here are some suggested answers:
  - **Protects the sheep**
  - **Leads them**
  - **Lays down his life for the sheep**
  - **Feeds them and leads them to still water**
  - **Owns the sheep**
  - **Finds lost ones**
  - **Knows the sheep and the sheep know him**
  - **Keeps them from going astray**
  - **They listen to his voice**
- Have them look at John 10:11 and 14. What kind of shepherd is Jesus? The Good Shepherd
- Summary: Jesus **laid down** His **life** for us. He **knows** us and we **know** Him. He is our **protector**.

Step 9   I Am the Resurrection and the Life—John 11:25–26

- When Jesus was preparing to raise Lazarus from the dead, He told Martha, Lazarus's sister, "I am the **resurrection** and the **life**. He who believes in me will

live, even though he dies; and whoever lives and believes in me will never die."
John 11:25–26

- Anybody can die. Jesus' Resurrection proves:
  - **He came from God**.
  - **What He claimed about Himself was true**.
  - **He is able to save us**.
  - **God is able to raise us from the dead also**.
  - **We can have life**.
- 1 Corinthians 15:12–23 The importance of the Resurrection
  - Jesus is the first fruits of resurrection; after Him, we are raised.
- John 10:10: "I have come that they may have life, and have it to the full."
- Summary: Jesus **raises** us from the **dead** and gives us **life**.

Step 10 I Am the Way, Truth, Life—John 14:1–6

- In John 13, Jesus begins a long discourse with His disciples as He prepares them for the Cross.
- Read John 14:1–6. Here, Jesus told His disciples that He was going to prepare a place for them. He told them that they knew the way to the place where He was going. Thomas said that they didn't know where He was going, so how could they know the way? Jesus answered, "I am the **way** and the **truth** and the **life**. No one comes to the Father except through me" (John 14:6).
- We can see the "the's": The way, the truth, the life.
  - Not **a** way, **a** truth, **a** life — not one way among others
  - Jesus doesn't say He will **show us** the way or **tell us** the truth or **give us** the life.
  - He said He **is** the way and the truth and the life.
- Notice also that He is the **only way** to the Father.
  - This contradicts the statement people make that there are many ways to God.
  - Similar to the Door of the Sheep—only one way in
- Summary: Jesus is the **only way** to the Father. He is the **truth**. He is the **life**.

Step 11 I Am the True Vine—John 15:1–17

- Look at John 15:1. Jesus is still teaching His disciples in preparation for the Cross. Here He says, "I am the **true vine**."
- Read John 15:1–8.
- What else does He say concerning the vine? Ask the students what they noticed. Below are some things they may notice.
  - **Jesus is the vine**. John 15:1
  - **His Father is the gardener**. John 15:1
  - **We are the branches**. John 15:5

- **He prunes the branches to make them more fruitful**. John 15:2
- **We are clean because of the word He has spoken to us**. John 15:3
- **We can only bear fruit if we are in the vine**. John 15:4–5
- **Our bearing fruit brings God glory and shows us as His disciples**. John 15:8
- If we remain in Him, we can ask for anything. John 15:7
- We remain in His love by obeying His commandments. John 15:10
- His commandment is that we love one another. John 15:12
- Summary: Jesus is the **vine** and we are the **branches**. We **produce fruit** when we **remain** in Him. When we are in Jesus, the Father **prunes** us to make us more **fruitful** so we can bring **glory** to Him.

Step 12 The Definition of *Eternal* or Full Life

- Many Scriptures, including several of the I AM statements, talk about life or eternal life.
- What is meant by this?
  - Life that is unending (John 5:24), but it is also more than this.
  - *The Holman Bible Dictionary* states: "The quality of life including the promise of resurrection which God gives to those who believe in Christ. . . . 'Quality of life' involves (1) life imparted by God; (2) transformation and renewal of life; (3) life fully opened to God and centered on Him; (4) a constant overcoming of sin and moral evil; and (5) the complete removal of moral evil from the person and from the environment of that person. . . . Since Christ is our life, we must make that life part of us by 'sharing in Christ,' by actively coming to Him and drawing life-giving strength from Him."
  - John 5:39–40: "You diligently study the Scriptures because you think that by them you possess eternal life. These are the Scriptures that testify about me, yet you refuse to come to me to have life."
  - John 17:3: "Now this is eternal life: that they may know you, the only true God, and Jesus Christ, whom you have sent."
    - "This knowledge is by experience—not from intellectual facts. Genuine knowledge of God by experience brings eternal life. Such experience transforms life." (*The Holman Bible Dictionary*)

Step 13 Summary

- Ask the students to look over their handouts and summarize what they have learned about Jesus from His "I AM" statements.

Step 14 Next Steps

- In the next lesson, we will begin to see what Christ did for us on the Cross.
- Pray.

Exodus 3:14: **I AM is God's name as He revealed it to Moses.** **YHWH**, the Lord

John 8:58–59
What does Jesus communicate with the statement in John 8:58–59?
- He is saying, **"I am God."**
- He states that **He existed before Abraham.**
John 1:3 states that Jesus is the **Creator**. (See also Genesis 1:26.)
Summary: Jesus is **God**.

John 6:25–35, 48–51
- John 6:26–27: Jesus told the people not to work for food that **spoils**, but for food that **endures** to eternal **life**.
- John 6:30–35: "I am the **bread** of **life**."
  What does it mean to "eat the bread of life"?

Week 7
Lesson 14
128

  - **"Eating the bread" means trusting the sacrifice He made for our sins and gaining eternal life.** John 6:29–30, 51, 54
  - **"Eating the bread" means feeding on the Word.**
    - **Spend time *in* the Word (the Bible).** John 6:63
    - **Spend time *with* the Word; Jesus is called the Word.** John 1:1
  - **"Eating the bread" means obeying the Father.** John 4:34
Summary: Jesus and His Word are our **spiritual food**.

John 8:12; 9:5
- John 8:12 and John 9:5: "I am the **light** of the **world**."
- When do we need light? When it is **dark**
Other references to light in the Bible: 1 John 1:5; Psalm 27:1; Psalm 119:105
- Once again, how do we experience Him as light? **In His Word**
Summary: Jesus **shows the way, reveals**.

John 10:7, 9
- John 10:7, 9: "I am the **gate** for the **sheep**."
What is the function of the gate?
- **Access—only way in**
- **Protection—shepherd only lets sheep in, not predators.**
Summary: Jesus is **the only way** in and is our **protection**.

John 10:11, 14

- John 10:11, 14: "I am the **Good Shepherd**."

What does a shepherd do for his sheep?

- **Protects the sheep; leads them; lays down his life for the sheep, feeds them**
- **Owns the sheep; finds lost ones; knows the sheep and the sheep know him; keeps them from going astray; speaks to them**

Summary: Jesus **laid down** His **life** for us. He **knows** us and we **know** Him. He is our **protector**.

John 11:25–26

- John 11:25: "I am the **resurrection** and the **life**."

Anybody can die. Jesus' Resurrection proves:

- **He came from God.**
- **What He claimed about Himself was true.**
- **He is able to save us.**
- **God is able to raise us from the dead also.**
- **We can have life.**

1 Corinthians 15:12–23: The importance of the Resurrection

- Summary: Jesus **raises** us from the **dead** and gives us **life**.

———ww———

John 14:1–6

- John 14:6: "I am the **way** and the **truth** and the **life**."
- Doesn't say He will **show us** the way or **tell us** the truth or **give us** the life
- Said He **is** the way and the truth and the life

He is the **only way** to the Father.

Summary: Jesus is the **only way** to the Father. He is the **truth**. He is the **life**.

John 15:1–17

- John 15:1: "I am the **true vine**."

What does He say concerning the vine?

- **Jesus is the vine.** John 15:1
- **His Father is the gardener.** John 15:1
- **We are the branches.** John 15:5
- **He prunes the branches to make them more fruitful**. John 15:2
- **We are clean because of the word He has spoken to us.** John 15:3
- **We can only bear fruit if we are in the vine.** John 15:4–5
- **Our bearing fruit brings God glory and shows us as His disciples.** John 15:8
- Summary: Jesus is the **vine** and we are the **branches**. We **produce fruit** when we **remain** in Him. When we are in Jesus, the Father **prunes** us to make us more **fruitful** so we can bring **glory** to Him.

The Cross

Stepping Stones

> ➢ Key Figure: Jesus
> ➢ Key Word: Sacrifice
> ➢ Key Concept: Jesus gave His life for us.
> ➢ Key Scriptures: Matthew 21:1–11; Matthew 26–27; references from Mark, Luke, and John

★ Teacher's Note

All of the Gospels contain the story of the Cross and the Resurrection. For the most part, the chronologies are the same, with minor differences and additions. For the sake of simplicity and to help the students be able to follow the story easily, we have used mainly the account found in Matthew, adding a few references where another Gospel writer had detail we wanted to include.

Be sure to pray for your students and for the class times before you teach this and the next two lessons. These lessons will be sharing what Jesus accomplished for us in His Cross and Resurrection. The lesson after these will call for a response to the gospel. Pray that the Holy Spirit will be at work in the students preparing them for salvation. Pray for the student's focus on the story and its implications. The enemy will try to distract them from the message of the gospel.

★ Important Teaching Notes

Handouts. This lesson would be best taught as a story, relating the important details of the Cross. Find lesson handouts for participants, available online.

We once taught it with the handout and much time was lost due to students getting confused and trying to fill in all the blanks on the handout. They were often distracted from the story by the need to complete the handout. When they would miss filling in a blank, they stopped listening until they could ask for it to be repeated, along with the three or four other blanks they had missed.

A better idea might be to share your Handout Key and let them follow along and make notes. The Handout Key provides a good outline for them to keep because it is the chronology of the Cross with Scripture references. Some students like to have this kind of resource for later study. And studying on their own is one of our goals for our students.

Reading. There is a lot of Scripture to be read in this lesson. We have noted the longer passages that you might want to read, to save time. If you do not have strong readers in your class, you may want to read more of the passages.

OVERVIEW

Lesson Objectives
- To see and appreciate the sacrifice Jesus made on our behalf for our sins.
- To see what other characters were involved and the roles they played.

Step 1   Introduction
- Pray—be sure to begin every lesson with prayer.
- Everything we have been studying leads up to this.
- Today we will look at the story of Jesus' Cross.

Step 2   Jesus' Last Week
- Triumphal Entry Matthew 21:1–11

  - The week before the Cross, Jesus entered Jerusalem for His last week.
  - Before He arrived in the city, He sent two disciples ahead to get a colt and bring it to Him.
  - He rode this **colt** into the city and was greeted by the people who praised Him and spread **branches** on the road before Him.
  - This was a **king's** welcome and fulfilled prophecy: "See your king comes to you . . . gentle and riding on a donkey, on a colt, the foal of a donkey" (Zechariah 9:9).
  - He was treated in a completely different manner at the end of the week.
- The week before the Crucifixion:
  - Jesus spent a busy week in Jerusalem ministering to the crowds and in various **conflicts** with the religious leaders.
- Jesus predicted His Crucifixion. Matthew 26:1–2
  - Just prior to the Cross, Jesus predicted His death on the Cross as He had done many times throughout His ministry.
  - The Cross was not a surprise to **Jesus** or to His **Father** in heaven. It was planned before time began. Acts 2:23; Revelation 13:8
  - As we will see later, it was also His choice.

Step 3   The Plot to Kill Jesus—Matthew 26:3–5, 14–16
- Have someone read John 11:45–48.
- Throughout most of Jesus' ministry, the Jewish rulers did not understand that Jesus had been sent by the Father. They saw him as a **threat** to the religious establishment and to their **power**. John 11:48

- In the past, Jesus eluded their grasp, because it was not yet His time. John 7:30; 8:20 But now, the hour had come. John 13:1
- Have someone read Matthew 26:3–5.
  - Most of the rest of the readings will come from the account in Matthew. Tell students to keep their Bibles open to this book.
- Now, the chief priests and elders plotted to **arrest** Jesus.
- Read Matthew 26:14–16. At this same time, one of Jesus' own disciples, Judas Iscariot, went to the chief priests and **offered** to deliver Jesus to them.
  - Iscariot is not Judas' last name.
  - It is a reference to where he is from: Kerioth.

Step 4   The Last Passover—Matthew 26:17–29
- Preparations for Passover Matthew 26:17–19
  - It was time to celebrate the Feast and Jesus' disciples asked Him where they should **prepare** to eat the Passover.
    - Remember, we discussed the Passover when we studied Moses.
  - Jesus gave them specific instructions and they found everything as He had said.

- The Last Passover, the Lord's Supper Matthew 26:20–29
  - This Passover meal was to be the last Passover, for Jesus was going to fulfill it through His death and Resurrection.
  - Prediction of Betrayal
    - While they were eating, Jesus predicted that one of them would betray Him.
    - In what was surely a tragic scene, each of the disciples asked if he was the one who would do it. Mark 14:19
    - But, no, Jesus said that Judas Iscariot was the one. Sometime later, Judas left, but the other disciples were confused about what he went to do. John 13:27–29
  - They had already celebrated the Passover in the usual manner, but then Jesus instituted the **Lord's Supper** where He gave new meaning to the elements of the meal.
  - Have someone read Matthew 26:26.
    - First He took the **bread**.
    - The bread represented His body, which would be broken for them on the Cross.
  - Have someone read Matthew 26:27–28.
    - Then He took the **cup**.
    - The cup represented His blood which would be shed for them, and us, on the Cross.

Step 5 Mount of Olives—Matthew 26:30–35

- After the meal, Jesus and His disciples went to the Mount of Olives.
- You will all fall away; you will deny me.
  - Have someone read Matthew 26:31–35.
  - Here Jesus told the disciples more about what would happen that night.
  - First, He predicted that they would all **fall away.**
  - Peter spoke up to defend himself, saying that he would never fall away.
  - But Jesus had more bad news for him. He told Peter that before a cock crowed, Peter would deny Him **three** times.
  - Again Peter disagreed and said he would **die** with Jesus but not deny Him.
  - Peter was not the only one talking this bravely. All the disciples said the **same** thing.

Step 6 Optional Step: Jesus' Last Words to His Disciples —John, Chapters 14–17

- John records several important final teachings that Jesus gave in His last night.

- These last teachings included the following:
  - Jesus comforted His disciples and told them that He is the way, the truth, and the life. John 14:1–6
  - He reminded them that He and the Father are one and that there would be power in His name when they prayed. John 14:7–15; 16:23–33
  - He told them about the Holy Spirit that He would send to them. John 14:16–26; 16:7–15
  - He comforted them and prepared them for what was coming. John 14:27–33; 16:1–6, 16–22
  - He taught them that He is the vine and they are the branches and they could not do anything except they were abiding in the vine. John 15:1–11
  - He talked to them about their relationship with each other and with the world. John 15:12–27
  - He concluded by praying a most amazing prayer to His Father giving us a glimpse of His prayer life and His relationship with the Father. We also hear Him praying directly for His disciples and for us. John 17

Step 7 Gethsemane—Matthew 26:36–46

- Read Matthew 26:36–46. (This is a long section. The teacher may want to read it, rather than assigning it to a student.)
- Jesus and His disciples entered a garden in the Mount of Olives called the garden of Gethsemane.

- Jesus was facing His most difficult time. To prepare Himself, He **prayed** in grief and anguish.
- Mark 14:36 tells us that when He was praying to His Father, He called Him "Abba, Father." This is a very personal name for father, similar to our word, **"Daddy."**
- Luke 22:43–44 tells us that when He began praying, an angel from heaven appeared and strengthened Him. It also tells us that He was in such anguish as He prayed that His sweat was like drops of **blood** falling to the ground.
- It is comforting to know that even Jesus needed to prepare Himself so that He could do the Father's will.
- Jesus went aside from the disciples **three** times to pray to His Father. Each time He came back to them, He found them **asleep**. His disciples, who also needed to be praying about what was coming, were not able to stay awake and pray. They would later fail because of this lack of preparation.

Step 8   Betrayal and Arrest—Matthew 26:47–56

- Read Matthew 26:47–56.
- When Jesus finished praying, Judas arrived with a **crowd** carrying swords and clubs sent from the chief priests and elders.
- Judas came up to Jesus and **kissed** Him. This was the sign that Jesus was the one they should arrest.
- Peter drew a sword and cut off the **ear** of the high priest's slave, whose name was Malchus. John 18:10 Jesus rebuked Peter and told him to put away his sword. Then He healed the slave.
- After Jesus was arrested, the disciples **fled** as predicted.

Step 9   Jesus before the Sanhedrin—Matthew 26:57–68

- What followed was a chaotic night.
- In violation of the Law, the chief priests met all night trying to find false testimony against Jesus, but they couldn't get the witnesses to agree.
- Through all of this, Jesus was **silent**.
- Have someone read Matthew 26:63–66.
- Finally, the high priest put Jesus under oath and asked Him directly, "Are you the Christ?"
- In His answer, Jesus quoted Daniel 7:13, which was a prophecy of the Messiah. The Jewish leaders did not miss the point. Now they were able to accuse Him of a crime—blasphemy—which is claiming to be **God**.
  - Note: Messiah and Christ are both terms for the promised anointed one. Messiah is Hebrew, Christ is Greek.
- With that charge, they could sentence Him to **death**.
- Then they spit in His face, struck Him with their fists, and mocked Him.

Step 10 Peter's Denials—Matthew 26:69–75
- Have someone read Matthew 26:69–75.
- While all this is going on inside, Peter was outside warming himself by a fire. Luke 22:55; Mark 14:67
- **Three** times he was questioned about his association with Jesus and **three** times he denied that he knew Him.
- Immediately after the third denial, a cock crowed, just as Jesus predicted.
- Luke 22:61 tells us that Jesus turned and looked at Peter. Imagine seeing that look.
- Peter **remembered** the word that Jesus had spoken earlier and realized what had just happened. He went out and **wept** bitterly.

Step 11 The Sentence of Death—Matthew 27:1–2
- In the morning, the Jewish leaders called a meeting of the Council. This Council was called the Sanhedrin and was the Jews' highest governing body.
- They sentenced Jesus to **death**, bound Him, and delivered Him to Pilate, who was the Roman governor in the area.

Step 12 Optional Step: Judas Regrets—Matthew 27:3–10
- When Judas saw that Jesus had been condemned to death, he felt remorse and tried to return the money to the religious leaders.
- They refused it.
- Judas then threw the money in the Temple and hanged himself.
- The religious leaders couldn't put blood money into the Temple treasury so they used it to buy a field to be used as a cemetery for strangers.

Step 13 Jesus and the Romans—Matthew 27:11–31
- Jesus Before Pilate (Herod, Pilate) Matthew 27:11–26
  - After Jesus was delivered to him, Pilate questioned Jesus, but he couldn't find any crime He had committed.
  - The Jewish leaders accused Jesus before Pilate, but again, Jesus was silent.
  - Pilate then stated that he could "find no basis for a **charge** against this man" (Luke 23:4).
  - Pilate was in a difficult place. His job was to keep the **peace** and this situation was clearly getting out of control. In a series of moves, he tried to defuse the situation.
    - First, he found out that Jesus was from Galilee, Herod's district. Herod was in town, so Pilate sent Jesus to him. After making sport of Him, Herod sent Jesus back to Pilate. Luke 23:5–12

- Next, Pilate told the Jews to judge Jesus according to their law, but they reminded him that by Roman law they weren't allowed to put a man to **death**. John 18:31–32
- Pilate's wife warned him to have nothing to do with "that innocent man" because she had a troubling dream about Him.
- Pilate then tried to release Jesus according to a custom where he released a prisoner during the festival. The Jewish leaders would have none of that and persuaded the crowd to ask for a **murderer**, Barabbas, instead.
- Finally, Pilate asked what he should do with "Jesus who is called Christ." The crowd shouted, "Crucify him!" When Pilate asked them why, they shouted even louder, "Crucify him!"
- Pilate realized he was not making any progress, so he:
  - Tried to wash his hands of innocent blood
  - Released Barabbas
  - Had Jesus flogged—scourged
    - ○ Scourged: whipped with a cruel whip
    - ○ This whip had pieces of metal and other sharp objects tied into the cords.
    - ○ These sharp pieces tore off flesh with every blow, sometimes leaving the victim nearly dead.
  - Turned Him over to be crucified
- Jesus and the Roman Soldiers Matthew 27:27–31
  - The Roman soldiers took Jesus into the Praetorium (the governor's hall).
  - Here they **mocked** Him.
    - They stripped Him and put a royal-looking **robe** on Him.
    - They made a **crown** out of thorns and pressed it into His head.
    - They put a reed scepter into His hand and mocked Him as a king.
  - After mocking Him, they led Him away to be crucified.

Step 14 Crucifixion—Matthew 27:33–46

- Read Matthew 27:33–46. (Another long section you, the teacher, may want to read.)
- The place where they crucified Him was called Golgotha (the Place of the Skull).
- After they crucified Him, the Roman soldiers divided up His **clothes** by casting lots (gambling). This was a fulfillment of Scripture: Psalm 22:18. Then they sat down to watch.
- Pilate had an inscription nailed to Jesus' Cross. It said, "This is Jesus, The King of the Jews."

- According to John 19:20–22, this phrase was written in Aramaic, Latin, and Greek, the major languages of the time.
- The Jewish chief priests took issue with the wording, but Pilate refused to change it.
- **Two** robbers were crucified with Him, one on the right and one on the left. This fulfilled the Scripture in Isaiah 53:9.
- As Jesus hung on the Cross, the crowd and the Jewish rulers **mocked** Him. They challenged Him to "save yourself."
  - But if He saved Himself, then He wouldn't save us, and that is why He came.
- Even the two robbers mocked Him.
  - According to Luke 23:39–43, one of the robbers defended Jesus.
  - In response to his faith, Jesus said that this robber would be in paradise with Him that very day. This shows that salvation is purely by faith. The thief on the Cross did not have time to earn his salvation, yet Jesus gave it to him on the basis of his faith.
- Jesus hung on the Cross for <u>six</u> hours, approximately 9 a.m. to 3 p.m. (Mark 15:25). From noon to 3 p.m. **darkness** covered the land, even though it was the middle of the day.
- At about 3 p.m., Jesus cried out with a loud voice, "My God, my God, why have you forsaken me?"

Step 15 Death and Aftermath—Matthew 27:50–54
- Have someone read Matthew 27:50–54.
- John 19:30 tells us that Jesus cried out, "It is **finished**!"
- Notice that when Jesus died, He gave up His spirit. His life wasn't **taken** from Him. He **gave** it. This was as planned and prophesied by God.
- Several extraordinary things happened as soon as Jesus died:
  - The curtain of the Temple was **torn** in two from top to bottom.
  - There was an earthquake.
  - Tombs opened up and bodies of holy people were raised. They went into the city and appeared to many people.
  - The Roman soldiers were frightened.
  - The centurion (Roman soldier) who was standing guard at the Cross said, "Surely he was the Son of God!" Quite a statement from an unbeliever.
- According to John 19:31–34, the Jews asked Pilate to break the legs of the crucified men so their bodies could be removed before the Passover, which would begin at sunset.
  - Breaking their legs would hasten the death of the men on the crosses.
  - Pilate agreed and the soldiers broke the legs of the two criminals. But when they came to Jesus they found that He was already dead, so they did not break His **legs**.

- To make sure He was dead, they pierced His **side** with a spear, and blood and water came flowing out.
- This was all in fulfillment of Scripture.
  - Psalm 34:20; Exodus 12:46; Isaiah 53:5; Zechariah 12:10

Step 16   Burial—Matthew 27:57–66
- Have someone read Matthew 27:57–61.
- Joseph, a rich man from Arimathea, went to Pilate and asked for the **body** of Jesus. Pilate consented.
- Joseph, with the help of Nicodemus (John 19:39), prepared the body for **burial**. They weren't able to complete the job because the Sabbath was coming. Luke 23:55–56
- Some of the women, who followed Jesus, saw where they had buried Him.
- Have someone read Matthew 27:62–66.
- The Pharisees **remembered** what Jesus said about rising on the third day and asked Pilate for a guard for the tomb.
- He told them they could have a guard posted and secure the tomb.

- They secured the tomb, posted a guard, and set a seal on the stone covering the entrance to the tomb.

Step 17   Next Steps
- In the next lesson we will look again at some of the Scriptures we have seen in past lessons and see how Jesus' death on the Cross fulfilled them.
- We will also see a little of what Jesus went through for us.
- Pray.

HANDOUT KEY: LESSON 15—THE CROSS

Jesus' Last Week
Triumphal Entry: The week before the Cross, Jesus entered Jerusalem for His last week. Matthew 21:1–11
- He rode a **colt** into the city and was greeted by the people who praised Him and spread **branches** on the road before Him.
- This was a **king's** welcome and fulfilled prophecy in Zechariah 9:9.
- Jesus spent a busy week in Jerusalem ministering to the crowds and in various **conflicts** with the religious leaders.
- Jesus had predicted His death on the Cross. Matthew 26:1–2
- The Cross was not a surprise to **Jesus** or to His **Father** in heaven. Acts 2:23; Revelation 13:8

The Plot to Kill Jesus—John 11:45–48; Matthew 26:3–5, 14–16

- The Jewish rulers saw him as a **threat** to the religious establishment and to their **power**. John 11:48
- The chief priests and elders plotted to **arrest** Jesus.
- At this same time, one of Jesus' own disciples, Judas Iscariot, went to the chief priests and **offered** to deliver Jesus to them.

The Last Passover—Matthew 26:17–29

- It was time to celebrate the Feast and Jesus' disciples asked Him where they should **prepare** to eat the Passover. Matthew 26:17–19
- They had already celebrated the Passover in the usual manner, but then Jesus instituted the **Lord's Supper** where He gave new meaning to the elements of the meal. Matthew 26:20–29
- First He took the **bread** which represented His body that would be broken for them on the Cross.
- Then He took the **cup** which represented His blood that would be shed for them on the Cross.

Mount of Olives—Matthew 26:30–35

- Jesus predicted that the disciples would all **fall away**.
- He told Peter that before a cock crowed, Peter would deny Him **three** times.
- Peter said he would **die** with Jesus but not deny Him.
- All the disciples said the **same** thing.

Gethsemane—Matthew 26:36–46

- To prepare Himself for His most difficult time, Jesus **prayed** in grief and anguish.
- He and his disciples entered the garden of Gethsemane.
- When Jesus was praying, He called His Father "Abba, Father." Mark 14:36
- This is a very personal name for father, similar to our word, "**Daddy**."
- Jesus was in such anguish as He prayed that His sweat was like drops of **blood** falling to the ground. Luke 22:43–44
- Jesus went aside from the disciples **three** times to pray to His Father.
- Each time He came back to them, He found them **asleep**.
- His disciples were not able to stay awake and pray.

Betrayal and Arrest—Matthew 26:47–56

- When Jesus finished praying, Judas arrived with a **crowd** carrying swords and clubs sent from the chief priests and elders.
- Judas came up to Jesus and **kissed** Him. This was the sign that Jesus was the one they should arrest.

- Peter drew a sword and cut off the **ear** of the high priest's slave. Jesus healed the slave.
- After Jesus was arrested, the disciples **fled** as predicted.

Jesus Before the Sanhedrin—Matthew 26:57–68
- Through all of the questioning, Jesus was **silent**.

Finally, the high priest asked Jesus directly, "Are you the Christ?" In His answer, Jesus quoted Daniel 7:13 which was a prophecy of the Messiah. The Jewish leaders did not miss the point.
- They accused Him of the crime of blasphemy, which is claiming to be **God**.
- With this charge, they could sentence Him to **death**.

Peter's Denials—Matthew 26:69–75
- **Three** times Peter was questioned about his association with Jesus.
- **Three** times he denied that he knew Him.

Immediately after the third denial, a cock crowed as predicted by Jesus.
- Peter **remembered** the word that Jesus had spoken earlier.
- He went out and **wept** bitterly.

The Sentence of Death—Matthew 27:1–2
The Jewish Council was called the Sanhedrin.
- They sentenced Jesus to **death**, bound Him, and delivered Him to Pilate, who was the Roman governor in the area.

Jesus and the Romans—Matthew 27:11–31
Jesus before Pilate   Matthew 27:11–26
- Pilate stated that he could "find no basis for a **charge** against this man" (Luke 23:4).
- Pilate's job was to keep the **peace**.
- The Jews reminded Pilate that they weren't allowed to put a man to **death**. John 18:31–32
- The Jewish leaders persuaded the crowd to ask to free a **murderer** named Barabbas instead of Jesus.

Pilate asked what he should do with "Jesus who is called Christ." The crowd shouted, "Crucify Him!"

Jesus and the Roman Soldiers   Matthew 27:27–31
- They **mocked** Him.
- They stripped Him and put a royal-looking **robe** on Him.

- They made a **crown** out of thorns and pressed it into His head.
- They put a reed scepter into His hand and mocked Him as a king.

Crucifixion—Matthew 27:33–46

The place where they crucified Him was called Golgotha (the Place of the Skull).

- After they crucified Him, the Roman soldiers divided up His **clothes**. Psalm 22:18
- Pilate had an inscription nailed to Jesus' Cross. It said, "This is Jesus, The King of the Jews."
- **Two** robbers were crucified with Jesus, one on the right and one on the left. Isaiah 53:9
- As Jesus hung on the Cross, the crowd and the Jewish rulers **mocked** Him.
- Jesus hung on the Cross for **six** hours, approximately 9 a.m. to 3 p.m.
- From noon to 3 p.m. **darkness** covered the land, even though it was the middle of the day.

At about 3 p.m. Jesus cried out with a loud voice, "My God, my God, why have you forsaken me?"

Death and Aftermath—Matthew 27:50–54

- Jesus cried out, "It is **finished**!" John 19:30
- When Jesus died, He gave up His Spirit. His life wasn't **taken** from Him. He **gave** it freely.
- The curtain of the Temple was **torn** in two from top to bottom.
- There was an earthquake.
- The centurion (Roman soldier) who was standing guard at the Cross said, "Surely he was the Son of God!"
- When the Roman soldiers came to Jesus and found that He was already dead, they did not have to break His **legs**. John 19:31–34
- To make sure He was dead, they pierced His **side** with a spear, and blood and water came flowing out.

This was all in fulfillment of Scripture: Psalm 34:20; Exodus 12:46; Isaiah 53:5; Zechariah 12:10.

Burial—Matthew 27:57–66

- Joseph, a rich man from Arimathea, went to Pilate and asked for the **body** of Jesus.
- Nicodemus helped Joseph prepare Jesus' body for **burial**.
- The Pharisees **remembered** what Jesus said about rising on the third day and asked Pilate for a guard for the tomb.
- They secured the tomb, posted a guard, and set a seal on the stone covering the entrance to the tomb.

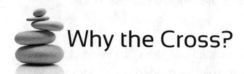

Why the Cross?

Stepping Stones

> ➢ Key Figure: Jesus
> ➢ Key Word: Fulfillment
> ➢ Key Concept: Significance of the Cross
> ➢ Key Scriptures: Various Old and New Testament passages

Note: Continue to pray for your students. In two lessons, you will be presenting the gospel. Find lesson handouts for participants, available online.

OVERVIEW

Lesson Objectives

- To show that Jesus willingly gave His life for us.
- To see what Jesus really went through for us.
- To show how Jesus fulfilled what the Old Testament said about Him.
- To show why the Cross was necessary.

Step 1 Introduction

- Pray—be sure to begin every lesson with prayer.
- Today we will discuss the significance of the Cross and show what Jesus really went through for us.

Step 2 Jesus Gave His Life

- It was not **taken** from Him. Ask someone to read John 10:17–18: "I lay down my life only to take it up again. No one takes it from me, but I lay it down of my own accord."
- Purpose: It was **why** He came.
  - Jesus said He did not come to be served, but to serve, and to give his life as a ransom for many. Matthew 20:28
  - Again, later, closer to the Cross, He said He would not ask the Father to save Him from the Cross because that was the reason He had come. John 12:27
- Jesus **predicted** His death.
  - Many times in His ministry, He specifically told the disciples details about His coming death on a cross and His resurrection three days later.

★ Teacher's Note

The following references are background information. You don't have to mention all these verses, but they are here in case you want them.

- Matthew 12:40; 16:4: Jesus likened His three days in the grave to the time Jonah spent in the fish.
- Matthew 16:21; Mark 8:31; Luke 9:22: "Who do men say I am?" He began to teach that the Son of Man must be rejected, killed, and rise again.
- Mark 9:31–32: Jesus told His disciples, but they didn't understand.
- Matthew 17:9: He told Peter, James, and John not to share about the transfiguration until after He had risen from the dead.
- Matthew 17:22–23: Jesus predicted His death and Resurrection; the disciples were deeply grieved.
- Matthew 20:17–19; Mark 10:32–34; Luke 9:51: We are going to Jerusalem; details of death.
- Luke 18:31–34 (rich young ruler): We are going to Jerusalem . . . they don't understand.
- Matthew 26:30–32: On the Mount of Olives just before His arrest, He told them to meet Him in Galilee after He would be raised.
- John 3:14; 8:28; 12:32: "If I be lifted up" (reference to being lifted up on a cross).
- John 10:11: I am the Good Shepherd. The Good Shepherd lays down His life for the sheep.
- John 12:23–25: The hour has come for the Son of Man to be glorified.

- They did not really <u>**understand**</u> what He was saying, as was later proved by their actions after the Cross.
- The Father had <u>**planned**</u> this from the beginning.
  - God planned and knew ahead of time that Jesus would die on a cross at the hands of wicked men. Acts 2:23
  - In Revelation, Jesus is called the "Lamb that was slain from the creation of the world" (Revelation 13:8).
    - Thus, in God's view, the Cross was a given from the beginning.
    - Remember Genesis 3:15?
- There was no <u>**other**</u> way.
  - Gethsemane (Matthew 26:36–46): Three times He prayed for another way.
  - There was no other way, so He submitted Himself to the Father.
- Jesus could have <u>**stopped**</u> the Crucifixion.
  - When the soldiers came to arrest Him in the garden, Jesus knew what was coming. He stepped forward and asked, "Who is it you want?" They

answered, "Jesus of Nazareth." When Jesus answered, "I am he," using God's covenant name, I AM, they drew back and fell to the ground. He had so much more power than even this band of soldiers and officers from the Pharisees. Jesus could have subdued them, but He allowed Himself to be arrested because He was submitted to the Father. John 18:4–6

- When He was arrested, He told Peter to put away his sword because He was able to ask the Father for 12 legions of angels (about 6,000 troops), but then the Scriptures would not be fulfilled. Matthew 26:52–56
  - In this same scene, He also asked, "Shall I not drink the cup the Father has given me?" John 18:11
- While He was on the Cross, the crowd taunted Him to "save yourself!" Matthew 27:39–43
  - He had the power to save Himself.
  - But, of course, He wouldn't do that because then He wouldn't save us.
- It is the greatest demonstration of God's **love**.
  - The Cross demonstrates God's love for us.
  - Have a student read 1 John 4:10.

  - "This is love; not that we loved God, but that he loved us and sent his Son as an atoning sacrifice for our sins."
  - Have another student read Romans 5:8.
    - "But God demonstrates his own love for us in this: While we were still sinners, Christ died for us."
  - Have the students turn to Romans 8:32.
    - J. I. Packer, in his book, *Knowing God*, quotes Romans 8:32 to show us that Jesus' gift on the Cross is our guarantee of all God's other gifts for us.
    - "This supreme gift is itself the guarantee of every other: 'He who did not spare his own Son, but gave him up for us all—how will he not also, along with him, graciously give us all things?'"

Step 3   What Jesus Went through for Us

- Discuss the significance of "the cup" in Jesus' Gethsemane prayer.
  - Review Gethsemane: Ask student participants to open their Bibles to Matthew 26:36–46. Note some of the details of His prayertime in Gethsemane, especially what He prayed and how distressed He was.
  - Why was Jesus so distressed about this night?
  - Author and Bible teacher Sara Margaret Wright discussed the reason. She asked the question, "What was 'the cup'?" that Jesus asked to be taken from Him?
  - Read her answer to the students. (This is also copied for them in their handouts.)

"Jesus the Christ was the pure and Holy One, untainted by sin. But He had come from Heaven to earth for only one purpose, and that was to take upon Himself the sin of every soul who ever lived—in the past, present, or future. That cup which, figuratively speaking, was being pressed to His pure lips, was full to the brim of man's iniquity. Into that cup, God the Father had poured the foul, filthy admixture of every heinous act committed under cover of the darkest night of earth by evil doers. Every demon-inspired and hellish sin of mortal man foamed and reeked in that cup. Yes, murder, adultery, cursing God's name, pride, selfishness, hate, covetousness, every evil, indeed, of which man's nature is capable went into the chalice. Must Jesus be brought into touch with such sin as had never touched His spirit, soul, or body? Must He take our guilt? God's answer was clear: 'There is no other way.'

"Had that been all, it would have meant acute torture for the Holy One. But that was only a part. The last bitter dregs of the cup were yet to be partaken, even 'the wine of the wrath of God'! God never condones sin; His anger is hot against evil in every manifestation. Each sin must be paid for. Then the Lord Jesus faced the hour when, on the Cross, He must be under the very curse of God for our sakes if we were to have our debt paid. . . . Father and Son had agreed upon the only possible remedy for the sin of mortal man, and the 'fullness of time' had come. Tomorrow loomed the Cross. . . . The Lord Jesus, His sweat like great drops of blood in His agony, prayed, 'Father . . . not My will, but Thine, be done.' He accepted the cup."

- Discuss what happened on the Cross.
  - Review Jesus' suffering.
    - After Jesus had been falsely accused, sentenced to a death He did not deserve, cruelly mistreated by mocking and scourging, crucified, and had hung on the Cross for six hours, three of those hours in darkness, He cried out, "My God, My God, Why have you forsaken Me?"
  - What did it mean when Jesus asked God, "Why have You forsaken Me?"
  - Again, Wright answers this question so well.
  - Read the following to the students. (Again, this is copied in the student handouts.)

"Our finite minds can but dimly discern what our Lord and Saviour did during those last three hours on the Cross. As the sun ceased to shine, Christ gave a great cry, saying, 'My God, My God, why hast Thou forsaken Me?'... He had 'laid upon Jesus the iniquity of us all.' The sin that went into 'the cup' was now being attributed to the sinless One. And in order that our full penalty might be paid, God poured out His wrath upon His beloved Son. In those dread hours — and we speak cautiously and reverently — God looked upon Jesus as though He were the vilest sinner who had ever lived.... Jesus went through the agony of a lost soul. In those hours He suffered the equal of an eternity in hell."

Step 4 It Is Finished!

- The end had come.
  - Our debt had been paid.
  - Jesus cried out once more, saying, "It is finished!" John 19:30
  - Then He yielded up His Spirit and died. Matthew 27:50
- "It is finished!" Jesus' last statement from the Cross is powerful, meaningful. He had finished the work God had sent Him to do.

- Jesus' "It is finished!" is translated from *tetelestai*, a word used in New Testament times, written on business documents or receipts to mean that a bill had been **"paid in full."** Jesus' work on the Cross completely paid for our sins. There is nothing we need to do to add to that work!
- Salvation is ours as a **gift** that we only need to accept by **faith**. Ephesians 2:8–9
- Author Watchman Nee said this:

   "Only with the atoning price paid could he cry: 'It is finished!' But because of that triumphant cry, the analogy we have drawn is a true one. Christianity indeed means that God has done every-thing in Christ, and that we simply step by faith into the enjoy-ment of that fact.... And the first lesson we must learn is this: the work is not initially ours at all, but his."

Step 5 Why Was Jesus' Sacrifice Necessary?

- Why couldn't God just snap His fingers and make us all reconciled?
  - When man sinned, a **debt** was created that must be paid.
  - God has been clear in His Word about the need for **blood** sacrifices to pay for sin, beginning with Adam and Eve.
    - What did Adam and Eve do when they saw God after they had sinned?
      ○ They hid from Him.
      ○ Even they knew that something had gone wrong, something was broken.

- Sin had **broken** the relationship with their **heavenly Father**. That sin required payment in order for them to be restored.
- What did God do?
  - He punished the couple and cursed the serpent who had deceived them. Genesis 3:14–19
  - He covered them with skins to replace the leaves they used. This required the death of an animal. Genesis. 3:21
  - He sent them out of the garden. Genesis 3:22–24
  - He promised a Savior. Genesis 3:15
- The **Law** given to Moses clearly shows that sin must be paid for by **blood**. God prescribed many sacrifices for sin in the Law that He delivered to Moses.
- The **New** Testament also shows that sin must be paid for:
  - Romans 3:23 says that all have sinned and fall short of the glory of God.
  - Romans 6:23 says that the wages of sin is death.
- Jesus is the **sinless** sacrifice (unblemished lamb) in the New Testament.
  - Point them to the handout: Moses's Story, Part 2—Passover. Note that John the Baptist, Paul, Peter, and John the Apostle identified Jesus as the Lamb.
  - The blood to pay for our sins can be our own or someone else's — but if it is someone else's, he must not have sins of his own to pay for.
  - Jesus is sinless and is able to pay for our sins.
    - Tell them to look at the first sentence of 1 Peter 3:18 while you read it. "For Christ died for sins once for all, the righteous for the unrighteous, to bring you to God."
  - On the Cross there was an exchange: our sin for His righteousness. Have someone read 2 Corinthians 5:21.
  - Romans 5:6 says that when we were still powerless (that is, when we were unable to pay our sin debt), Christ died for the ungodly.
  - Romans 6:23 also says that the gift of God is eternal life in Christ Jesus our Lord.

Step 6 Old Testament Scripture Fulfilled in Jesus' Cross
- Jesus' death on the Cross is the fulfillment of all that we have seen God do and promise throughout this chronological Bible study.
- Remember Genesis 3:15?
  - The seed of the woman's heel has been struck.
  - The head of the serpent has been crushed.
- Remember Abraham's answer to Isaac's question?
  - God Himself will provide the lamb for the sacrifice.
  - The Lamb has been slain.
- Remember Passover?

- Ask students what they remember about Passover, which was taught in the lessons on Moses.
  - God brought Israel out of slavery in Egypt using ten plagues to force the Pharaoh to let them go.
  - The last of the 10 plagues was the death of the firstborn.
  - God protected Israel using the Passover. They put lamb's blood on door-posts, which would cause the Angel of Death to "pass over" their houses.
- Have students go back to Moses's Story, Part 2 handouts. Look at the bottom of the handout on the Passover. Note again the parallels between Jesus and the Passover lamb.
  - Core Bible Stories (see bradleybaptist.org) notes these reasons the soldiers did not break Jesus' legs:
    - Jews would not allow crucified men to be left to die during their day of rest, the Sabbath.
    - Crucified people could hang from crosses for many days before dying. Breaking their legs usually made them die quickly since they could not push themselves up to breathe, when their position on the Cross — hanging from their arms — made it extremely difficult to do so.

    - Jesus was already dead after only six hours on the Cross. That gives us another indication of the kind of beating He had suffered before being crucified.
  - One of our students added that Jesus probably died quickly because He had to become sin and experience the full weight of God's wrath. He *gave* His life.

Step 7 The Curtain of the Temple Was Torn When Jesus Died

- Review: Tabernacle. Review the handout of the picture of the Tabernacle given in Moses's Story, Part 2. Especially note the Holy Place and the curtain separating it from the Most Holy Place.
- Ask someone to read Matthew 27:51.
- *"In verse 51, we read that once Jesus yielded up His spirit, the veil was torn in two. It should first be noted that the veil initially represented the separation between us and God. The Israelites originally had been commanded to meticulously organize the Tabernacle according to God's instructions and 'hang the veil from the clasps . . . and bring the ark of the Testimony in there, behind the veil. The veil shall be a divider for you between the holy place and the Most Holy' (Exodus 26:33 NKJV). So, when we see that Christ's crucifixion split the veil, the purpose of His death is exemplified. . . . It is through these events that Christ allowed us the opportunity to come into fellowship with God."*

—Amanda's devotional, "The Purpose of Christ's Crucifixion"

- Note that the veil was torn from **top** to bottom. Who tore it? **God**
  - The Father agreed, "It is finished."
  - The price has been **paid**.
  - The way to heaven is now **open**.
- The Tabernacle was a picture of **heaven**. Hebrews 8:5
  - The high priest entered the Holy of Holies once a year with the blood of goats and calves to offer sacrifice for his sins and the sins of the people.
  - Jesus entered **heaven** itself with His own **perfect** blood to offer sacrifice for our sins **once** for all mankind and forever. Hebrews 9:11–12
  - Point students to "Why so specific?" on "The Tabernacle" page of Moses's Story, Part 2 handout.
  - Teachers may also want to see Hebrews 8–10 for more detail.
- Have someone read Hebrews 4:14–16. Now we can come **boldly** before the throne of God through Jesus, our High Priest.

Step 8   Our Response to the Cross
- The Cross calls for a response from us.
- Read this modern day parable:

> "There is a story of a little boy who, with his own hands, made a small toy boat. It was his own workmanship, and was therefore very dear to him. Each day he played with it on the shore of the lake near his home; each evening he anchored it safely at the water's edge. But one night it slipped its moorings and sailed away. In the morning the boy was dismayed to learn that he had lost his boat. Every effort to recover it proved unavailing. The boat was gone. Some days later his father took him into town several miles down the shore. While walking through the streets, in a shop window the lad spied a boat. 'Daddy!' he cried with glee, 'That's my very own boat!' It was, indeed, easily recognizable as his own handiwork. They entered the store and the little boy said to the shopkeeper, 'Sir, that little boat is the one I made then lost. Would you give it back to me?' But the man replied, 'I cannot give you the boat, my boy, but I will sell it to you.' And eagerly the little fellow produced the purchase price. Then joyfully clasping the small craft in his arms, he headed for home with his daddy.
>
> "How strange a situation it would have been, had the boat looked up into the boy's face and said, 'I do not belong to you!' For it was twice his, indeed. He had first made it himself, and then, when it was lost, he had bought it back again. O soul, dare you look into the loving face of Jesus and say, 'You have no right to

my life'? First, He created you for His own; then, when by sin you went astray, He paid the full price for your redemption. Rightly, you are twice His. But, differently from the boat, we have a will of our own. We can choose to remain unsaved and go straight to hell. Or we can choose to accept the Lord Jesus Christ as our Redeemer, and know the joy of His salvation. 'Wilt thou be made whole?' Will you accept the Christ of Calvary?"

—SARA MARGARET WRIGHT

★ Application to Life

Bradleybaptist.org puts it this way:

You have all the information you need about Jesus to make a decision.

Who is Jesus to you? Head knowledge is not enough. You must get to know Him personally, experientially. What are you going to do with what you know? Are you going to submit to Him or do you prefer to "live your life" without Him? Are you going to follow Him or are you going to deny Him in your life?

Lack of a response to this is a response.

Step 9 Next Steps

- In the next lesson we will see Jesus' victory on the Cross in His Resurrection.
- Jesus will show His disciples how His Cross and Resurrection fulfilled Scripture.
- Pray.

HANDOUT KEY: LESSON 16—WHY THE CROSS?

Jesus *Gave* His Life

- It was not **taken** from Him. John 10:17–18
- It was **why** He came. Matthew 20:28
- Jesus **predicted** His death, but the disciples did not really **understand** what He was saying.
- The Father had **planned** this from the beginning. Acts 2:23
- There was no **other** way. Matthew 26:36–46
- Jesus could have **stopped** the Crucifixion. Matthew 26:52–56
- It is the greatest demonstration of God's **love**. Romans 5:8; 8:32

What Jesus Went through for Us

Why was Jesus so distressed in the garden of Gethsemane? Bible teacher Sara

Margaret Wright discussed the reason, asking, "What was 'the cup'?" that Jesus asked to be taken from Him?

> *"Jesus the Christ was the pure and Holy One, untainted by sin. But He had come from Heaven to earth for only one purpose, and that was to take upon Himself the sin of every soul who ever lived — in the past, present, or future. That cup which, figuratively speaking, was being pressed to His pure lips, was full to the brim of man's iniquity. Into that cup, God the Father had poured the foul, filthy admixture of every heinous act committed under cover of the darkest night of earth by evil doers. Every demon-inspired and hellish sin of mortal man foamed and reeked in that cup. Yes, murder, adultery, cursing God's name, pride, self-ishness, hate, covetousness, every evil, indeed, of which man's nature is capable went into the chalice. Must Jesus be brought into touch with such sin as had never touched His spirit, soul, or body? Must He take our guilt? God's answer was clear: 'There is no other way.'*
>
> *"Had that been all, it would have meant acute torture for the Holy One. But that was only a part. The last bitter dregs of the cup were yet to be partaken, even 'the wine of the wrath of God'! God never condones sin; His anger is hot against evil in every manifestation. Each sin must be paid for. Then the Lord Jesus faced the hour when, on the Cross, He must be under the very curse of God for our sakes if we were to have our debt paid . . . . Father and Son had agreed upon the only possible remedy for the sin of mortal man, and the 'fullness of time' had come. Tomorrow loomed the Cross. . . . The Lord Jesus, His sweat like great drops of blood in His agony, prayed, 'Father . . . not My will, but Thine, be done.' He accepted the cup."*

What happened on the Cross? What did it mean when Jesus asked God, "Why have You forsaken Me?" Again, Sara Margaret Wright answers this question so well.

> *"Our finite minds can but dimly discern what our Lord and Saviour did during those last three hours on the Cross. As the sun ceased to shine, Christ gave a great cry, saying, 'My God, My God, why hast Thou forsaken Me?' . . . He had 'laid upon Jesus the*

iniquity of us all.' The sin that went into 'the cup' was now being attributed to the sinless One. And in order that our full penalty might be paid, God poured out His wrath upon His beloved Son. In those dread hours — and we speak cautiously and reverently — God looked upon Jesus as though He were the vilest sinner who had ever lived. . . . Jesus went through the agony of a lost soul. In those hours He suffered the equal of an eternity in hell."

It Is Finished!
- The word Jesus used that is translated "It is finished!" is a word that means "**paid in full**."
- Salvation is ours as a **gift** that we only need to accept by **faith**. Ephesians 2:8–9

Why Was Jesus' Sacrifice Necessary?
Why couldn't God just snap His fingers and make us all reconciled?
- When man sinned, a **debt** was created that must be paid.

- God has been clear in His Word about the need for **blood** sacrifices to pay for sin, beginning with Adam and Eve.
- Sin had **broken** the relationship with their **heavenly Father**. That sin required payment in order for them to be restored.
- The **Law** given to Moses clearly shows that sin must be paid for by **blood**.
- The **New** Testament also shows that sin must be paid for.
- Jesus is the **sinless** sacrifice (unblemished lamb) in the New Testament.
  - 1 Peter 3:18; 2 Corinthians 5:21

—⚍—

Old Testament Scripture Fulfilled in Jesus' Cross
Review Passover. See Passover handout from Lesson 8—Moses's Story, Part 2.

_____

_____

The Curtain of the Temple Was Torn When Jesus Died
Review the Tabernacle. See Tabernacle handout from Lesson 8—Moses's Story, Part 2.
- See Matthew 27:51. Note that the veil was torn from **top** to bottom. Who tore it? **God**.
- The price has been **paid**.
- The way to heaven is now **open**.
- The Tabernacle was a picture of **heaven**. Hebrews 8:5

- Jesus entered **<u>heaven</u>** itself with His own **<u>perfect</u>** blood to offer sacrifice for our sins **<u>once</u>** for all. Hebrews 9:11–12
- Now we can come **<u>boldly</u>** before the throne of God through Jesus, our High Priest. Hebrews 4:14–16

Our Response to the Cross

You have all the information you need about Jesus to make a decision.

Who is Jesus to you? Head knowledge is not enough. You must get to know Him personally, experientially. What are you going to do with what you know? Are you going to submit to Him or do you prefer to "live your life" without Him? Are you going to follow Him or are you going to deny Him in your life?

Lack of a response to this is a response.

(source: bradleybaptist.org)

The Resurrection

Stepping Stones

> ➢ Key Figure: Jesus
> ➢ Key Word: Victory!
> ➢ Key Concept: Jesus rises from the dead. The prophecies are fulfilled.
> ➢ Key Scriptures: Luke 24

Note: Continue to pray for your students. The lesson after this is the gospel presentation. Find lesson handouts for participants, available online.

OVERVIEW

Lesson Objectives

- To rejoice that Jesus rose from the dead.
- To see that now the Scriptures are fulfilled. All that God has been planning and promising in His Word has been fulfilled.

Step 1   Introduction

- Pray—be sure to begin every lesson with prayer.
- Today we will look at Jesus' Resurrection.
- Now it really *is* finished. The Resurrection shows that Jesus has completed the work God sent Him to do.
- Victory is ours through Jesus!

Step 2   The Tomb Is Empty!

- A look back; set the stage.
  - The disciples have followed Jesus for three years.
  - They thought He was the One, the Messiah promised by God for so long.
  - They were hoping that He was the one who would save Israel.
  - But He had been delivered up by their leaders and cruelly crucified on a cross by the Romans.
  - Because the Sabbath was approaching, they didn't even have time to give Him a proper burial.
  - So in grief and mourning, the women came to the tomb after the Sabbath to anoint the body of Jesus and say their final good-byes.

154

- Imagine what it was like.
  - Imagine, after all that has happened, the state they were in and what they were expecting to find.
  - Remember also that Jesus had told them what would happen, but they had not understood.
- Have someone read Luke 24:1–12.
  - Now, imagine their thoughts and reactions when they find it completely different than they had expected.
- They are looking for a dead body.
  - What did the women bring with them?
    - The women came to the tomb with **spices** because they were planning to finish the embalming that had to be rushed before Jesus' burial because the Sabbath was approaching. Luke 23:54–56
  - They were surprised that the stone has been rolled away from the entrance to the tomb.
    - On the way to the tomb they had been discussing who would roll away the stone for them. Mark 16:3
  - When they entered the tomb, they were looking for a **body**, not a risen Savior.
- He is risen!
  - They saw two men in gleaming clothes who are later identified as angels. Luke 24:23
  - The men asked the women why they were looking for the living among the dead.
  - Then they told the women the most amazing news: "He is **not here**; he **has risen!**"
    - What! Is it possible? Is it too good to be true?
  - The angels reminded them that Jesus had told them He would be crucified and then rise on the third day.
  - They remembered Jesus' words.
  - They ran to tell the disciples who couldn't believe what they were hearing.
  - Imagine the stir this news caused among Jesus' friends and disciples, even among the whole city of Jerusalem—disbelief, excitement, fear, hope, and more.
- Optional topic: Encounters with the women
  - All of the Gospels mention that the women were the first to arrive at the tomb and that the stone had already been moved.
    - Matthew, Mark, and Luke mention one or two angels.
    - John says that Mary Magdalene saw Jesus at the tomb.
  - It is surprising that the story shows the women arriving first, considering the status of women at that time.

- But it is no surprise when you consider how Jesus treated women all through His ministry.
- Also, it is no surprise when you remember the love and faithfulness shown by the women throughout Jesus' life on earth.
  - Even at the Cross, Luke tells us that they followed the body of Jesus to see where He was buried and then went home to prepare spices before they rested on the Sabbath. Luke 23:55–56
- You may want to watch the Resurrection scenes from the film *Magdalena: Through Her Eyes*. The end of this film shows the reaction of the disciples and the women to Jesus' Resurrection and concludes with a presentation of the gospel that includes an explanation of why Jesus had to die, a summary of biblical history and Jesus' ministry, and a scene where a skeptical woman is led to faith in Jesus. (You may want to save this clip for Lesson 18.)

Step 3   The Road to Emmaus—Luke 24:13–35

- Ask for volunteers for the five characters in the Road to Emmaus Drama. (See handout available online.)
  - Have your "actors" (volunteers) read the story of the two who traveled to Emmaus and met Jesus on the way.
  - Or you could read the passage in an animated way if you choose.
- Why were two disciples leaving town?
  - The two disciples were returning home after the Passover and the Sabbath.
- Jesus came up from behind, so they assumed that He had been in Jerusalem also.
- They began a conversation with Jesus, but they were clearly disappointed and disillusioned with what had happened.
  - This is even in the face of the evidence they knew about.
  - Look at Luke 24:19–24.
    - Jesus, the one they hoped would save Israel, had been crucified.
    - It was now the third day and some amazing things were occurring.
      - How many times had Jesus said to them that He would rise on the third day?
      - Some women had been to the tomb and did not find His body, but did see angels who said He was alive and reminded them of His words.
      - Others had gone to the tomb and verified their story.
  - They did not realize that Jesus had taken on our final enemy, death. They saw Jesus' death as final and they had lost hope.
- First, Jesus rebuked them for being foolish and slow of heart.
  - One definition of being *foolish* is not seeing things from God's perspective.

- This can happen to us too.
  - Let it not be said of us that we were foolish and slow of heart to believe all that the prophets have spoken about Jesus!
- Jesus told the two travelers that the Christ had to **suffer** these things.
  - This is what we have been studying in this chronological Bible study.
  - God has been getting the world ready for His Messiah beginning with His promise of a Savior in Genesis 3:15.
  - He continued through the promises He made to the patriarchs (Abraham, Isaac, Jacob), to King David, and to others.
  - He gave more detail about the role of the Messiah through the Law He gave through Moses.
  - He also spoke about His Promised One in the prophecies and warnings of the prophets.
  - This is what Jesus was explaining to the travelers in Luke 24:27.
    - God predicted this from the beginning and now it has come to pass.
    - Jesus has fulfilled all that God promised for us, to save us.
  - Wouldn't you like to have been at *that* Bible study?
- After they arrived at their destination, Jesus acted like He was planning to travel further, but Cleopas and his friend urged Jesus to stay the night with them.

- When they ate the evening meal, Jesus gave thanks and broke the bread and gave it to them. Their eyes were **opened** and they recognized Jesus. Then He disappeared.
  - Jesus has broken bread for the disciples many times before. What events are described in these two passages?
    - Luke 9:16: Jesus blessed the loaves and fishes before He multiplied them for the five thousand.
    - Luke 22:19: Jesus broke the bread and gave thanks at the Last Passover, Lord's Supper, just before going to the Cross.
  - Luke 24:31 says their eyes were opened.
    - Luke 24:16 says they were kept from recognizing Jesus as they walked on the way to Emmaus. Here are some possible reasons for this.
      - This may be because they weren't expecting to see Jesus, even though they had already heard reports that He was alive. They thought He was dead.
      - They were unwilling to see Him. Their hearts were not right for seeing. They had lost hope.
      - Maybe God closed their eyes so this conversation could take place. It was a teachable moment. (God has done similar things in the past. He hardened Pharaoh's heart so He could show His glory to Israel and Egypt in the Exodus. See also Isaiah 6:9–10; Mark 4:10–12.)

- Maybe something about Jesus' breaking the bread and blessing it triggered a memory. Maybe God opened their eyes.
- After Jesus disappeared, they said that their hearts were **burning** when He was explaining the Scriptures to them.
  - Note that their hearts were burning within them even before they knew that it was Jesus talking to them.
  - This is the effect that the Word of God has.
  - Hebrews 4:12 says that "the word of God is living and active. Sharper than any double-edged sword, it penetrates even to dividing soul and spirit, joints and marrow; it judges the thoughts and attitudes of the heart."
  - Have someone read Isaiah 55:10–11. This passage says that God's Word accomplishes His purposes.
  - Through the Holy Spirit we can have the same experience today that these two disciples had on the road to Emmaus. First John 2:27 says His anointing teaches us about all things and is real and not counterfeit.

Step 4   Jesus Appeared to the Disciples

- Have someone read Luke 24:33–43.
- Imagine their excitement now. The two disciples have returned to Jerusalem and before they can even begin their story they hear that others have actually seen Jesus too.
- Imagine this conversation as they excitedly shared with one another, talking fast, daring to believe.
- Then to prove it is true, Jesus stood among them. All talking ceased and they were startled and frightened.
- What did they think they were seeing? They thought He was a ghost.
- He reassured them and showed them that He was not a **ghost**. He used all of the five senses—**hearing, sight, touch, smell**, and **taste**. Do you see it?
  - First, He spoke to them.
  - He told them to look at His hands and feet to see that it is, indeed, Jesus.
    - ○ What would they have seen by looking at His hands and feet? Nail holes.
  - Then, He invited them to touch Him.
    - ○ What would they learn by touching Him? That His body was real.
  - Lastly, to confirm it in their minds, He asked for a piece of fish, which they could smell.
  - Then He ate the fish in front of them.
    - ○ What would this prove? He was not a ghost; ghosts don't eat.
- How do they react? Luke 24:41 says they can't believe it because of joy and amazement. It *is* that good and it is *true*!

Step 5 The Scriptures Had to Be Fulfilled

- Have someone read Luke 24:44–46.
- Now Jesus began to teach them.
- He said again, this time to all of the disciples, that the Scriptures had to be **fulfilled**.
  - The three categories He mentions — the Law of Moses, the Prophets, and the Psalms — correspond to the three Jewish divisions of the Old Testament.
- This time He opened their **minds** to understand the Scriptures. Now they would understand what they did not understand before the Cross.
- He had told them that He must suffer and rise again on the third day many times before, but they had not understood.
  - This is why they came to the tomb looking for a dead body.
  - This is why they didn't believe when others said they had seen angels and an empty tomb, or even Jesus Himself.
  - This is why they didn't recognize Jesus when He spent a whole day traveling with them.
  - Now they have seen Him and He has opened their minds. Now, they will begin to understand what Jesus has accomplished through His death and Resurrection, what God planned from the beginning.

Step 6 Go and Tell

- Have someone read Luke 24:47–49.
- Now there is a job to be done. He is preparing them for the work He has for them. The **Good News** must be told.
- Jesus has died and risen from the dead three days later as prophesied. Now, repentance and forgiveness of sin are available to the nations.
- He reminded them that they are witnesses of **these things**.

★ Application to Life

When we know Jesus as Savior, we are witnesses also.
Repentance and forgiveness must still be proclaimed in His name to people we meet.

- But He tells them to wait for what the Father has promised, **the Holy Spirit**. He told them not to begin until they were clothed with **power** from on high.
- Jesus left them. Luke 24:50–53
  - These last verses probably took place later.
  - Jesus appeared to various people and groups (1 Corinthians 15:5–7) over a period of time (probably 40 days). Then He ascended to heaven.

- Verses 49–53 get us ready for Luke's sequel, the Book of Acts, where he tells about Jesus' last words, His ascension, His sending of the Holy Spirit, and the growth of the church.

Step 7 Summary

- The Resurrection was a most important event.
- Anyone can **die**. Other religious groups have prophets, but they are all dead. Our Savior is alive.
- The Resurrection shows that the sacrifice Jesus made on the Cross was **accepted**. The work He came to do was **completed**.
- It fulfills prophecies made about Jesus.
- Bradleybaptist.org attests, "It is our guarantee that Jesus is who He said He is and that He has the power and authority to do what He said He would do."

★ Application to Life

Read 1 Corinthians 15:12–20.

Here, Paul shows the importance of the Resurrection.

He says that if Christ is not raised then our preaching is in vain and so is our faith. 1 Corinthians 15:14

He says our faith is worthless and we are still in our sins. 1 Corinthians 15:17

Jesus' Resurrection is our **guarantee** that believers in Jesus will one day be resurrected. 1 Corinthians 15:20

Step 8 Next Steps

- Play a song or sing a hymn that celebrates the Resurrection.
  - Suggestions: Nicole C. Mullen's "Redeemer" or Natalie Grant's "Alive"
- In the next lesson, we will have to decide what to do about this salvation that Jesus has made possible through His Cross and Resurrection.
- Pray.

HANDOUT KEY: LESSON 17—THE RESURRECTION

The Tomb Is Empty!
- The women came to the tomb with **spices**. Luke 24:1
- They were looking for a **body**, not a risen Savior.
- The angels told the women the most amazing news, "He is **not here**; he **has risen!**" Luke 24:6

The Road to Emmaus

- Jesus told the two travelers that the Christ had to **suffer** these things. Luke 24:26
- Their eyes were **opened** when Jesus broke the bread and gave it to them. Luke 24:31
- After Jesus disappeared, the two travelers said that their hearts were **burning** when He was explaining the Scriptures to them. Luke 24:32

Jesus Appeared to the Disciples

- Jesus appeared to the disciples. He showed them that He was not a **ghost**. Luke 24:39
- He used all of the five senses: **hearing, sight, touch, smell,** and **taste.**

The Scriptures Had to Be Fulfilled

- Jesus said the Scriptures had to be **fulfilled**. Luke 24:44
- He opened their **minds** to understand the Scriptures. Luke 24:45

Go and Tell

- The **Good News** must be told.
- Jesus said they are witnesses of **these things**. Luke 24:48
- But He tells them to wait for what the Father has promised, **the Holy Spirit**.
- He told them not to begin until they were clothed with **power** from on high. Luke 24:49

Summary

- The Resurrection was a most important event.
- Anyone can **die**. The Resurrection shows that the sacrifice Jesus made on the Cross was **accepted**. The work He came to do was **completed**.
- Jesus' Resurrection is our **guarantee** that believers in Jesus will one day be resurrected. 1 Corinthians 15:20

The Good News—
The Ultimate Choice

Stepping Stones

> Key Figure: Sinners
> Key Word: Responding
> Key Concept: God's offer of salvation requires a response from us.
> Key Scriptures: Romans 3:23; 6:23; John 3:16; Romans 5:8; John 14:6; Romans 10:9–10

OVERVIEW

Lesson Objectives

162

- To present the gospel and call for a response.
- This is the climax of this Bible study.
- Goals
  - Define salvation.
  - Answer the question, "How can I find salvation?"
  - Show that Jesus is the only way.
  - To have students understand and accept the gospel.

Step 1   **Begin the Lesson**

- Pray—be sure to begin every lesson with prayer.
- We have seen and discussed the sacrifice that Jesus made for us on the Cross and how He rose in fulfillment of Scripture.
- It is not enough to know this. It requires a decision from us.

Step 2   **Review**

- Review the stories you have covered so far in this Bible study and show the evangelistic message. Show God's progressive revelation of Himself from the Old Testament through the New Testament.
  - God created man.
  - Man fell.
  - God immediately offered a Savior.
  - God chose a family—Abraham.
  - God made promises to the family and repeated them to successive generations.

- God began to fulfill the promises.
  - Joseph was a blessing to the nations around Egypt, not just Egypt or Israel.
- God gave the Law.
- God made more promises.
  - Such as promise of an eternal kingdom to David
- Ultimate fulfillment of all the promises was in Jesus, beginning with His birth and on through to the Cross and Resurrection.
- Review Jesus' story briefly. Ask them what meant the most to them.
- Implications for us
  - All of this brings the question: "What does this mean for us?"
  - There is a choice to be made.

Step 3   Systematic Gospel Presentation

- Present the gospel to the students using some systematic approach that you are comfortable with.
- Some suggestions:

  - Evangecube
  - *Four Spiritual Laws* by Bill Bright
  - The Roman Road: four things a person needs to know to be saved:
    - He is a sinner. Romans 3:23; 3:10
    - He must pay for sin. Romans 6:23
    - Christ paid the price for him. Romans 5:8 (also John 3:16)
    - He must repent and trust Jesus. Romans 10:9;13
  - Ephesians 2:1–10: The plan of salvation
    - Before—We were dead in our sins. Ephesians 2:1–3
    - God provided a way. Ephesians 2:4
    - After—We were made alive. Ephesians 2:5–7
    - Now—What we are. Ephesians 2:8–9
    - Now—What we do. Ephesians 2:10
      - Note that we are not saved *by* works, but *for* works.
  - Homemade tract
- Provide some kind of tract that students can follow as you present the gospel. There are resources on the Internet where you can purchase tracts and other resources for the Evangecube, the *Four Spiritual Laws*, and others if you use those plans. Make your own tract or your own plan with Scripture.
- You may want to play the end of the movie, *Magdalena: Through Her Eyes*. It has a wonderful gospel presentation given to a woman who appears skeptical and feels unworthy.
- Suggestion: Teachers could give their testimonies. Or you might allow other students to give theirs if they are willing.

- After the gospel has been presented, give an invitation. Consider playing some worship or evangelistic hymns and offering private time with anyone who would like to pray or ask questions.
  - Suggestion: Play the song "In Christ Alone" as this song does a great job of communicating the gospel and its effect on our lives. You may want to find the words on the Internet and pass them out so the students can follow along.

Step 4 What Happens Next?

- If appropriate, celebrate with students who have made decisions. Don't embarrass anyone. You may want to ask for their permission to share what has happened to them.
- Cover what happens after salvation (prayer, reading the Bible, finding a Bible-teaching church, and so on).
- In tracts, this is usually covered after the prayer.
- Encourage new believers to find a Bible-teaching church and to begin to be discipled.

Step 5 Summary

- We have seen how God has worked all through history to provide us with a way to come back to Him.
- Jesus' Cross and Resurrection is God's offer to us. This requires a choice by us, to accept His offer or to reject it. This choice has eternal consequences.

Step 6 Next Steps

- Accepting Jesus' offer of salvation from sin is only the beginning.
- In the next two lessons we will see how the gospel changes a life when we look at the lives of Peter and Paul.
- Pray.

How the Gospel Changes a Life—Peter

Stepping Stones

> ➢ Key Figure: Peter
> ➢ Key Word: Impulsive or Bold
> ➢ Key Concept: God changes Peter from a rash and impulsive man to a brave and bold man.
> ➢ Key Bible Books: The Gospels and Acts

OVERVIEW

Lesson Objectives

- To look at Peter's life after he is changed by Christ.

165

Step 1   Begin the Lesson

- Pray—be sure to begin every lesson with prayer.
- Today we will see how a rash, impulsive, sometimes cowardly man is changed into a brave and bold man.
- We will see how knowing Jesus transformed Peter's character into one who is effective in the kingdom of God.

Step 2   Review

- The past few weeks we have been talking about Jesus.
  - We learned a little about who He was and what He did and said.
  - We talked about His Cross and Resurrection.
  - We talked about the decision required of us because of His offer of salvation.
- Recap the gospel message. Ask if anyone would like to share or has questions.
- We noted that asking Jesus to save us is only the beginning. When Christ comes into a life, that life changes.
- Now we will look at two men who were radically changed when they turned to Christ and gave Him their lives.
- In this lesson we will discuss Peter, one of Jesus' disciples, and in the next lesson we will look at Paul, a Jewish leader who started out persecuting the church, but God had other plans for him.

Step 3   Who Peter Was

- Read each of the following sets of verses. Have them write down and discuss what they discover about Peter's character in each of these passages. Answers given here are suggestions.
- We meet Peter early in Jesus' ministry.   Luke 5:1–11
    - **A fisherman**
    - **Spoke his mind**
    - **Knew he was a sinful man when confronted by Jesus' deity**
        - **Caught a load of fish after catching nothing all night**
    - **Jesus called him to follow, and Peter left everything.**
    - **Obedient**
- Peter walked on water, briefly.   Matthew 14:25–31
    - **Brave**
    - **Impulsive**
    - **Willing to risk, but unable to deliver**
    - **Little faith**
    - **Fear**

- **First to declare Jesus is the Messiah**   Matthew 16:13–20
- He began to understand what Jesus was about.
- **But he followed that with a statement that showed he didn't understand what that meant.**   Matthew 16:21–23
    - **He tried to dissuade Jesus from the path the Father had set out for Him.**
    - **Jesus rebuked Peter and told him that he didn't have the things of God in mind.**
    - **Peter was trying to fight a spiritual battle with the flesh.**
- Just before the Cross:
    - **Washing of the feet—John 13:5–10—Peter told Jesus to wash his whole body.**
        - **Wanted all Jesus had to give**
    - **Peter declared he would follow Jesus to the death.**   Mark 14:27–31
        - **Brave**
        - **Proud**
    - **He was corrected by Jesus for cutting off Malchus's ear** (servant of the high priest).   John 18:10–11
        - **Impulsive**
        - **Rash**
        - **He still didn't understand exactly what Jesus was doing even though Jesus told him He had to die.**
- Ask the students to summarize, "What kind of man was Peter?"

Step 4   Peter's Downfall

- Peter said he would follow Jesus to death, but Jesus predicted that he would deny Him three times. Mark 14:27–31
- Peter denied Jesus as predicted. Luke 22:54–62
  - Note that Jesus turned and looked straight at Peter. Luke 22:61
  - Imagine seeing that look!
  - That was when Peter remembered what Jesus had said to him.
  - What did he do then?
    - **He went outside and wept bitterly.**
- Imagine how Peter was feeling.
- What kind of man have we seen him to be? **Brave, proud, impulsive**
- What does this denial mean?
  - **He is not the man he thought he was.**
  - **He abandoned his Lord at the most critical moment.**
  - **He is disappointed in himself.**
  - **He may wonder if there is any way to get back.**
  - **Fear**

Step 5   Peter's Salvation, Restoration

- But there is a way back. Let's see how tenderly Jesus restored him.
- In Luke 22:31–32, **even before his denial, Jesus prayed for Peter and gave him both a hope that he will return and a purpose when he does: "Strengthen your brothers."**
- In Mark 16:7, **when the angel was speaking to the women at the tomb, he singled out Peter as if to say, *yes, Peter, even you.***
- In a scene after the Resurrection in John 21:1–22, Jesus restored Peter and gave him a new purpose.
  - Verses 1–8: **Peter was fishing and encountered Jesus. He responded to Him in his impulsive fashion.**
  - Verses 15–17: **Jesus told Peter to feed His sheep, a reference to caring for His people.**
    - Note that Jesus asked Peter three times if he loved Him.
    - This is the same number of times that Peter denied Jesus.
  - Verses 18–22: **Jesus also predicted Peter's death by crucifixion. When Peter looked back and asked what about another disciple, Jesus replied that was not Peter's business. He was to follow Jesus.**

Step 6   A New Character

- Jesus returned to heaven and told the disciples to wait in Jerusalem for the promised Holy Spirit.

- At Pentecost, the Holy Spirit fell on the disciples and **Peter gave a sermon** to the crowd who had witnessed this amazing event.
- In this sermon, Peter said some surprising things. Acts 2:22–24
  - "Men of Israel, listen to this: Jesus of Nazareth was a man accredited by God to you by miracles, wonders and signs, which God did among you through him, as you yourselves know. This man was handed over to you by God's set purpose and foreknowledge; and **you, with the help of wicked men, put him to death by nailing him to the Cross.** But God raised him from the dead, freeing him from the agony of death, because it was impossible for death to keep its hold on him."
- He **repeated a similar line on two more occasions**.
  - Acts 3:11–19: In his second sermon after he healed a lame man (full story Acts 3:1–26) Peter accused them of denying and killing the Christ and called them to repentance.
  - Acts 4:10: In his defense before the Jewish leaders after he was arrested for proclaiming the name of Jesus (full story in Acts 4:1–12) Peter said, "It is by the name of Jesus Christ of Nazareth, whom you crucified but whom God raised from the dead, that this man stands before you healed."

- This is the man who, when challenged, denied Jesus and said he never knew Him. **But here, in front of the same people, he bravely accused them of crucifying the Messiah.**
- What was the result?
  - After his first sermon, Acts 2:37–41: **They were cut to the heart and 3,000 people were saved.**
  - After healing the lame man, Acts 4:4: The number of men grew to 5,000.
- **This is not the same Peter we saw before the Cross. God has done a mighty work in him.**
  - **He used the boldness and impulsiveness of his character for the kingdom.**
  - **Peter got it.**
  - **He stood up to the ones he once feared.**

Step 7   What About Us?

★ Application to Life

When God saves us, we do not **remain** the **same**.

He begins a process of conforming us to the **likeness** of His **Son**. Romans 8:29

Romans 12:1–2 says, "**offer** your bodies a **living sacrifice** . . . do not **conform** any longer to the **pattern** of this **world** . . . but be **transformed** by the **renewing** of your **mind**."

What renews our mind? God's Word

It is a process that takes work by <u>us</u> and by <u>God</u>. Philippians 2:12b–13

Just as Peter was emboldened by the <u>Holy Spirit</u>, God gives believers the power by His <u>Holy Spirit</u> to do what He calls us to do.

Note: Be careful not to give the impression that salvation is by works. It is by faith alone in Christ alone.

Ephesians 2:8–10 makes it clear that we are saved by grace through faith *for* good works.

Step 8   Summary
- When God saves a person, that person's life changes.
- God took Peter's character and transformed him, making him an effective servant for His kingdom.

Step 9   Next Steps
- Peter was a simple fisherman before he encountered Jesus. In the next lesson, we will see how Jesus changed the life of Paul, a Pharisee.
- Pray.

HANDOUT KEY: LESSON 19—HOW THE GOSPEL CHANGES A LIFE—PETER

Look at these passages. What do they reveal about Peter's character?

Luke 5:1–11
- <u>A fisherman; Spoke his mind; Knew he was a sinful man when confronted by Jesus' deity</u>
- <u>Jesus called him to follow and he left everything; Obedient</u>

Matthew 14:25–31
- <u>Brave; Impulsive; Willing to risk, but unable to deliver; Little faith; Fear</u>

Matthew 16:13–23
- <u>First to declare Jesus is the Messiah.</u> Matthew 16:13–20
- <u>But he followed that with a statement that showed he didn't understand what that meant.</u> Matthew 16:21–23
- <u>He tried to dissuade Jesus from the path the Father had set out for Him.</u>

- Jesus rebuked Peter and told him that he didn't have the things of God in mind.
- Peter was trying to fight a spiritual battle with the flesh.

John 13:5–10
- Washing of the feet — John 13:5–10 — He told Jesus to wash his whole body.
- Wanted all Jesus had to give

Mark 14:27–31
- He declared he would follow Jesus to the death. Mark 14:27–31
- Brave; Proud

John 18:10–11
- He was corrected by Jesus for cutting off Malchus's ear. John 18:10–11
- Impulsive; Rash
- He didn't understand exactly what Jesus was doing even though Jesus told him He had to die.

Peter denied Jesus as predicted. Mark 14:27–31
What does he do immediately after the denial? Luke 22:54–62
- He went outside and wept bitterly.
Imagine how Peter was feeling. What kind of man have we seen him to be?
- Brave, proud, impulsive
What does this denial mean?
- He is not the man he thought he was.
- He abandoned his Lord at the most critical moment.
- He is disappointed in himself.
- He may wonder if there is any way to get back.
- Fear

There is a way back. Let's see how tenderly Jesus restored him.
Luke 22:31–32 Jesus gave hope before the denial.
- Even before his denial, Jesus prayed for Peter and gave him both a hope that he will return and a purpose, "strengthen your brothers," when he does.
Mark 16:7 An angel singled him out.
- When the angel was speaking to the women at the tomb, he singled out Peter as if to say, *yes, Peter, even you*.
John 21:1–22 Jesus lovingly restored him.
- Peter was fishing and encountered Jesus. He responded to Him in his impulsive fashion.
- Jesus told Peter to feed His sheep, a reference to caring for His people.

- Jesus also predicted Peter's death by crucifixion. When Peter looked back and asked what about another disciple, Jesus replied that was not Peter's business. He was to follow Jesus.

Peter is a new man in Christ.

How do his actions at Pentecost differ from his actions before the Cross? What were the results?

- At least three times after the Cross, Peter accused the crowd of killing God's Messiah. Acts 2:22–24; Acts 3:11–19; Acts 4:10

  This was the man who, when challenged, denied Jesus and said he never knew Him. But here, in front of the same people, he bravely accused them of crucifying the Messiah.
- The result is that they were cut to the heart and people were saved. Acts 2:37–41
- This is not the same Peter we saw before the Cross. God has done a mighty work in him.
- He used the boldness and impulsiveness of his character for the kingdom.
- He got it.
- He stood up to the ones he once feared.

What about us?

- When God saves us, we do not **remain** the **same**.
- He begins a process of conforming us to the **likeness** of His **Son**. Romans 8:29

Romans 12:1–2 says:

- **Offer** your bodies as a **living sacrifice**.
- Do not **conform** any longer to the **pattern** of this **world**.
- But be **transformed** by the **renewing** of your **mind**.

It is a process that takes work by **us** and by **God**. Philippians 2:12*b*–13

- Just as Peter was emboldened by the **Holy Spirit**, God gives us the power by His **Holy Spirit** to do what He calls us to do.

How the Gospel Changes a Life—Paul

Stepping Stones

- ➤ Key Figure: Paul
- ➤ Key Word: Passionate
- ➤ Key Concept: God changes Paul's passion.
- ➤ Key Bible Books: The Book of Acts; some of Paul's letters

OVERVIEW
Lesson Objective

- To see how Paul changes after he encounters Christ.

Step 1   Begin the Lesson

- Pray—be sure to begin every lesson with prayer.
- Paul was a passionate man.
- Early in his life, unbeknownst to himself, his passion was directed against God's kingdom.
- We will see how Jesus transformed Paul's passion and gave him a special task to build His kingdom.

Step 2   Review

- We looked at the life of Jesus and learned who He was and what He came to do for us on the Cross.
- We saw that the Cross presented us with a choice to accept His sacrifice for our sins and be reconciled to God, or not.
- We saw that when we choose Jesus and He comes into a life through salvation, that life changes.
- We looked at the difference Jesus made in the life of Peter, a simple fisherman who was one of Jesus' disciples.
- In this lesson, we will see how Jesus changed a Pharisee named Saul.
  - Saul's name was later changed by God to Paul.
- Saul was a Jewish leader who started out persecuting the church, but God had other plans for him.

Step 3   Who Paul Was

- We meet Saul early in the church's history.
- "Stephen, a man full of God's grace and power," was doing "great wonders and miraculous signs among the people." Acts 6:8
- However, certain men who opposed Christianity argued with Stephen, but they could not stand up against his wisdom or the Spirit. Acts 6:9–10
- So they accused him falsely and stirred up the people and the elders and the teachers of the law. They brought him before the Sanhedrin (Jewish Council) and brought false witnesses against him. Acts 6:12–14
- They questioned Stephen and after he had given a long history of the people of Israel that ended with him accusing them of killing the Messiah, the people dragged him out and stoned him to death. Acts 7:1–60
- **Saul was on the sidelines, watching over their coats while they killed the first Christian martyr**. Acts 7:58
- Look at Acts 8:1. **He was also giving his approval to Stephen's death.**
- Note: Paul was also called Saul. Acts 13:9

Step 4   Paul's Downfall

- Soon after Stephen's death, a great persecution began against the church in **Jerusalem**.
- Read Acts 8:1–3. This was when "Saul began to **destroy the church**. Going from house to house, he dragged off men and women and put them in prison."
- Read Acts 9:1–2. In a short time, it was not enough to persecute the church only in Jerusalem. Saul went to the high priest and got letters so he could go to **Damascus** and bring Christians back to Jerusalem as prisoners.
- But God had other plans.

DISCUSS PAUL'S CHARACTER BEFORE HE MET CHRIST
What kind of man do you think Saul was before he met Jesus? • Let students give their thoughts. One suggestion: **A passionate man**
Look at how he described himself at that time of his life. Philippians 3:4–6 • **Put confidence in the flesh** • **Circumcised according to the Law** • **An Israelite** • **Of Benjamin's tribe** (second son of Jacob's favorite wife; Joseph's brother) • **A Hebrew of Hebrews** • **A Law-abiding Pharisee** • **So zealous he even persecuted the church** • **Faultless in his adherence to the Law**

And again: Galatians 1:13–14
- **Intensely persecuted the church and tried to destroy it**
- **Advancing in Judaism beyond other Jews his age**
- **Extremely zealous for the traditions of his fathers**

How did Saul think he would be saved?
- **By following the Law**

Step 5 Paul's Salvation, Restoration
- Read Acts 9:1–16.
- How did Jesus identify Himself to Saul?
    - **I am Jesus, whom you are persecuting.**
- He told Saul to **"get up and go into the city, and you will be told what you must do."** (Note that Paul had to obey first, just like Abraham when God called him.)
- What plans did God have for Saul?
    - Saul was His **"chosen instrument to carry his name before the Gentiles and their kings and before the people of Israel."** Acts 9:15
    - He would also **suffer for Jesus' name.** Acts 9:16
- How unlikely is this assignment for the man we described above, a Pharisee and a leader of the Jews?
    - **Paul, being a good and devout Jew, would have thought that Gentiles were no better than dogs (Matthew 15:26), yet God wanted him to take His precious gospel to them.**
    - **He was also to tell Israel this good news. Paul had formerly persecuted this message, to the delight of the Jews.**
    - **Paul had been persecuting the church, now he would be persecuted by Jews and Gentiles for the same thing, telling the good news of Jesus Christ.**

Step 6 A New Character
- Read or summarize Acts 9:19–30.
- The change in Paul is immediate. Within a few days, **he began to preach** in Damascus. The people were surprised, and probably wary, and they asked whether he was the one who was persecuting the church in Jerusalem and had come with letters to do the same in Damascus.
- He **kept on preaching, grew more powerful, and baffled the Jews who decided to kill him.**
    - This seems to be a pattern with them. They killed Jesus, then Stephen, and then went after Paul.
- He escaped them when his followers lowered him in a basket through an opening in the wall. Acts 9:19b–25

- He went to Jerusalem and tried to join the disciples there, but they didn't trust him. A man named Barnabas (meaning "son of encouragement") vouched for him and told them how Paul preached in Damascus.
- He **continued to speak fearlessly and boldly in Jerusalem,** but he **angered some Jews** who **decided to** (guess what?) **kill him.** To protect him, the church sent him to Tarsus.
- This pattern of going into a town, preaching boldly, and drawing the anger of the Jews plagued Paul throughout his ministry. At one point in his letters, he cited the many times and ways he had been persecuted. 2 Corinthians 11:23b–33

DISCUSS PAUL'S CHARACTER AFTER HE MET JESUS

Now look at how Paul described himself after his salvation. Philippians 3:7–14
Before his salvation, what was he depending on to make him right with God?
- **The Law; his own good works**
After his salvation, how did he look at all that? Philippians 3:7–8
- **Loss, rubbish**

Week 10
Lesson 20
175

What was he counting on for salvation? Philippians 3:9
- **Having a righteousness that comes through faith in Christ; not his own righteousness**
- The righteousness that comes from God and is **by faith**

What did he value? Philippians 3:8–11
- **Knowing Christ Jesus his Lord** Philippians 3:8
- **Gaining Christ** Philippians 3:8
- **Being found in Him** Philippians 3:9
- **Knowing Christ and the power of His Resurrection** Philippians 3:10
- **The fellowship of sharing in His sufferings**
- **Becoming like Him in His death**
- **To attain the resurrection from the dead** Philippians 3:11

How was he living his life? Philippians 3:12–14
- **Does not consider himself perfect** Philippians 3:12
- **Nor that he has attained that for which Christ has taken hold of him**
- **He presses on toward the goal to win the prize for which God called him.** Philippians 3:14
- **Forgets what lies behind** Philippians 3:13
- **Strives toward what is ahead** Philippians 3:13

How did he see himself? Galatians 1:15–16; 2:20 and Ephesians 3:8

- **Set apart by God from birth** Galatians 1:15
- **Called by God's grace** Galatians 1:15
- **Crucified with Christ** Galatians 2:20
- **No longer alive; Christ lives in him** Galatians 2:20
- **Lives by faith in the Son of God** Galatians 2:20
- **The least of all God's people** Ephesians 3:8
- **And yet, a preacher to the Gentiles** Ephesians 3:8

- Here is how Peter described Paul and his writings: 2 Peter 3:15–16
  - our dear brother, Paul
  - wrote with the wisdom that God gave him
  - His letters contain some things that are hard to understand, which ignorant and unstable people distort as they do the other Scriptures.
    - note that Peter calls Paul's writings "Scripture"

Step 7   **What About Us?**

★ Application to Life

- It doesn't matter **who we are**, whether we are poor fisherman or religious leaders, we all need **to be saved**. Romans 3:23
- When we believe in Jesus Christ, our sins are forgiven, we are reborn spiritually and God begins a mighty work in us.
- He makes us **new creatures** in Christ.
- "Therefore, if anyone is in Christ, he is a new creation; the old has gone, the new has come!" 2 Corinthians 5:17
- We are crucified with Christ and He lives in us and through us. Galatians 2:20

Step 8   **Summary**

- We have finished our chronological tour of the Bible.
- We saw how God created us for relationship, but mankind sinned and broke this relationship with God.
- But God was prepared. He would send a Messiah to pay the price for our sins and reconcile us to God.
- Jesus is God's Son and is God. He paid the price for sin on the Cross.
- His Resurrection proved that He was the one to make the payment for our sins.
- If we will believe in Him, we will be saved (reconciled to God).

- But we will not stay the same. God will begin a work in us to conform us to the image of His Son. Romans 8:29

Step 9 Next Steps
- Ask the students if they have anything to share or questions to ask about the course.
- Pray for them as they continue on their journey with God.

HANDOUT KEY: LESSON 20—
HOW THE GOSPEL CHANGES A LIFE—PAUL

When we first met Saul, where was he and what was he doing? Acts 7:54–58; Acts 8:1
- <u>Saul was on the sidelines, watching over their coats while they killed the first Christian martyr.</u> Acts 7:58
- <u>He was also giving his approval to Stephen's death.</u> Acts 8:1

What did Saul begin to do to the church? What city was he in? What other city did he travel to in order to do the same thing? Acts 8:1–3; 9:1–2
- <u>Saul was in Jerusalem. He began to persecute the church.</u>
- <u>He also went to Damascus to do the same thing there.</u>

What kind of man was Saul before he met Jesus? Philippians 3:4–6; Galatians 1:13–14
- <u>A passionate man</u>

How he described himself:
- <u>Philippians 3:4–6: Put confidence in the flesh; Circumcised according to the Law;</u>
- <u>An Israelite; Of the tribe of Benjamin; A Hebrew of Hebrews; A law-abiding Pharisee;</u>
- <u>So zealous he even persecuted the church; Faultless in his adherence to the Law</u>
- <u>Galatians 1:13–14: Intensely persecuted the church and tried to destroy it; Advancing in Judaism beyond other Jews his age; Extremely zealous for the traditions of his fathers</u>
- <u>Saul thought he would be saved by following the Law</u>

When Saul met Jesus, how did Jesus identify Himself to Saul? Acts 9:5
- <u>I am Jesus, whom you are persecuting.</u>

What does Jesus tell Saul to do? Acts 9:6
- "<u>Get up and go into the city, and you will be told what you must do.</u>"

What plans did God have for Saul (who was also called Paul, Acts 13:9)?
Acts 9:15–16
- <u>Saul is His "chosen instrument to carry His name before the Gentiles and their</u>
  <u>kings and before the people of Israel."</u> Acts 9:15
- <u>He would also suffer for Jesus' name.</u> Acts 9:16

How unlikely is this assignment for the man we described above, a Pharisee and
a leader of the Jews?
- <u>Paul, being a good and devout Jew, would have thought that Gentiles were no</u>
  <u>better than dogs (Matthew 15:26), yet God wanted him to take His precious</u>
  <u>gospel to them.</u>
- <u>He was also to tell Israel this good news. Paul had formerly persecuted this</u>
  <u>message, to the delight of the Jews.</u>
- <u>Paul had been persecuting the church, now he would be persecuted by Jews</u>
  <u>and Gentiles for the same thing, telling the good news of Jesus Christ.</u>

How did Paul show that he was different? Acts 9:19–30 One way people know
we have been saved is when we begin to act differently. (Matthew 7:16a "By their
fruit you will recognize them.")
- <u>He began to preach. He kept on preaching, grew more powerful, and baffled</u>
  <u>the Jews who decided to kill him.</u>

Now look at how Paul describes himself after his salvation.
Before his salvation, what was he depending on to make him right with God?
- <u>The Law; his own good works</u>

After his salvation, how did he look at all that? Philippians 3:7–8: <u>Loss, rubbish</u>
What was he counting on now for salvation? Philippians 3:9:
- <u>Having a righteousness that comes through faith in Christ; not his own</u>
  <u>righteousness</u>

What did he value? Philippians 3:8–11
- <u>Knowing Christ Jesus his Lord; gaining Christ, being found in Him;</u>
- <u>Knowing Christ and the power of His Resurrection;</u>
- <u>The fellowship of sharing in His sufferings; becoming like Him in His death;</u>
- <u>To attain the resurrection from the dead</u>

How was he living his life? Philippians 3:12–14
- **Does not consider himself perfect**
- **Nor that he has attained that for which Christ has taken hold of him**
- **He presses on toward the goal to win the prize for which God called him**
- **Forgets what lies behind; strives toward what is ahead**

How did he see himself now? Galatians 1:15–16; 2:20 Ephesians 3:8
- **Set apart by God from birth; called by God's grace; crucified with Christ**
- **No longer alive; Christ lives in him; lives by faith in the Son of God**
- **The least of all God's people; and yet, a preacher to the Gentiles**

What about us?

It doesn't matter **who we are**, whether we are poor fisherman or religious leaders, we all need **to be saved**. Romans 3:23

When we believe in Jesus Christ, our sins are forgiven, we are reborn spiritually, and God begins a mighty work in us.
- He makes us **new creatures** in Christ.

2 Corinthians 5:17: "Therefore, if anyone is in Christ, he is a new creation; the old has gone, the new has come!"

We are crucified with Christ and He lives in us and through us.

Galatians 2:20: "I have been crucified with Christ and I no longer live, but Christ lives in me. The life I live in the body, I live by faith in the Son of God, who loved me and gave himself for me."

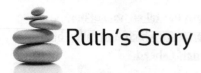

Ruth's Story

Stepping Stones

> ➤ Key Figure: Ruth
> ➤ Key Word: Provision
> ➤ Key Concept: God cares for His people.
> ➤ Key Bible Book: Ruth

Note: If this lesson is used, it should be presented in chronological order with the other lessons. Ruth's story should be taught before David's story. Find lesson handouts for participants, available online.

OVERVIEW

Lesson Objectives

● To see how God provides for His people.

Step 1   Begin the Lesson

● Pray—be sure to begin every lesson with prayer.
● Ruth is David's great-grandmother.
● Her story shows us the history of David's family.
● It also shows God's faithfulness to Israel and His mercy to the Gentiles.

Step 2   Review

● We have been studying the descendants of Abraham and seeing how God has been working out His plan of salvation.
● Israel is about to make a transition from a theocracy (God as leader) to a monarchy (a king as leader).
● Ruth is David's great-grandmother (Ruth 4:13–22), so her story is part of Israel's history.
● Ruth is also a Gentile. Here we get a glimpse into God's plan to save the whole world. Ruth is in Jesus' family line. Matthew 1:1, 5–16

Step 3   Introduction

● Give a brief history of the Book of Ruth.
  ● Ruth takes place at the end of the period of the judges, just before the monarchy.

- There is a famine in the land of Israel. Famines were devastating and sometimes families had to move to another place to survive.
- One of God's provisions for the poor was gleaning. This was stipulated in the Law. When they were harvesting their fields, God's people, Israel, were not to harvest to the corners nor were they to go back over the fields to pick up what was dropped. The poor were allowed to go into the fields after the harvesters had finished and pick up what was left behind.

Step 4   Group Work
- Split the class into four groups.
- Assign a chapter of Ruth to each of the groups.
- Give the students copies of the Ruth handouts.
- Tell the groups how much time they have (10 minutes; more time, if possible).
  - They should spend some time skimming the chapter individually (about three minutes).
  - Then they should work together for the remainder of the time (about seven minutes) looking at the chapter, filling in the chart, and discussing what they find.
  - Tell them they won't find something for each box or category in every chapter.
  - They should focus on the Word (what the Bible says), not opinion.

Optional Lesson 1
181

Step 5   The Chart—Filled Out
- The Handout Key for this lesson is a filled-out version of the chart the students will be working on.
- Teachers may want to do this exercise on their own to be familiar with the book and to generate this chart on their own.
- The chart they create and the one in the Handout Key are for the teacher only. Let the students discover the Word for themselves.
- Teachers should be prepared to supply information to help them discuss if needed.

Step 6   Discussing What They Learned
- After the time is up, discuss the categories in the large group. Discuss what we learn about the characters in the story, and what God was doing in their lives and in the bigger picture.
- Summarize the character of the main persons in the story.
  - Naomi
  - Ruth
  - Boaz

- Ask what was God doing? What was the big picture?
- How did the people involved fit into God's plan?

Step 7 Summary

- In Ruth's story we see how God cared for His people through circumstances and through His Law.
- Even though Ruth was a Gentile, she was willing to cast her lot with God's people and trust Him with her future.
- God set up the society so He could care for the people, but the people had to cooperate with His plan in order to be included in the blessings.

Step 8 Next Steps

- Introduce the next lesson you are planning to teach.
- Pray.

HANDOUT KEY: OPTIONAL LESSON 1—RUTH'S STORY

Chapter 1

Naomi's Character	Ruth's Character
v. 3 After Elimelech died, stayed in Moab with her sons **v. 7** Daughters-in-law willing to follow her **v. 8** Had nothing to offer; she releases them **vv. 11–13, 15** Trying to do her best for her sons **v. 18** Knows when to hush **v. 20** Wanted to be called Mara (bitter) instead of Naomi (pleasant)	**vv. 14, 16–17** Shows great love for and commitment to her mother-in-law (leaving her country and family to go to a foreign land with a *woman* who had *nothing* to offer) Also showed commitment to Naomi's God
Boaz's Character	**God's Provision — What, How**
(Not introduced in the book yet)	God provided Ruth to Naomi **v. 6** The famine had ended in Israel and God was providing for His people. **v. 22** When they arrive in Israel, the harvest is beginning.

Blessings — What, Who	Other Details
v. 9 Naomi blesses Ruth and Orpah.	**v. 1** In the days when the judges ruled **v. 1** Famine in the land **v. 2** Elimelech and his family were from Bethlehem Ephrathah (where the Messiah would be born Micah 5:2). **v. 2** They went to Moab to escape the famine. **v. 3** Elimelech dies. **v. 4** Sons marry Moabite women, Ruth and Orpah **vv. 4–5** After ten years, sons die. **v. 6** Naomi decides to return to Judah (Israel)

Chapter 2

Naomi's Character	Ruth's Character
vv. 20–22 Naomi is not just sitting expecting others to care for her. She is teaching Ruth and planning. She realizes that Ruth is gleaning in the field of a close relative. She offers Ruth good counsel to stay with Boaz for protection and provision.	**v. 2** Shows respect/honor to Naomi by asking her permission **v. 2** Willing to work; offered to work for Naomi **v. 7** Polite **v. 10** Humbled by Boaz's care **v. 13** Thankful **vv. 7, 17** Hard worker **vv. 14, 18** Provides for and shares lunch with Naomi **v. 23** Listens to and obeys Naomi; gleans with Boaz through the barley and wheat harvests; lives with her mother-in-law

Boaz's Character	God's Provision — What, How
v. 4 Man of faith; good relationships with his workers **vv. 8–16** Kind to Ruth; protects her while she gleans; provides for her; leaves extra for her **v. 11** Notices her sacrifice and commitment **v. 14** Invites Ruth to each lunch with him	Gleaning — how the Law provided for the poor **v. 3** Ruth happens to glean in Boaz's field

Blessings — What, Who	Other Details
v. 4 Boaz and his workers exchange blessings **v. 12** Boaz blesses Ruth; asks God to repay her for what she has done; prays for rich reward from Him since she trusted Him **v. 19** Naomi blesses Boaz again	**v. 1** Boaz is Naomi's kinsman of Elimelech's family; a man of great wealth

Chapter 3

Naomi's Character	Ruth's Character
v. 1 Naomi wants to provide security for Ruth **vv. 2–4** Naomi proposes a plan to Ruth **vv. 16–18** Relationship between Naomi and Ruth	**vv. 5–6** Submissive to Naomi's plan; "obeyed" Naomi **v. 10** Willing to marry an older man **v. 11** Boaz and others know her as a woman of noble character

Boaz's Character	God's Provision — What, How
vv. 11, 13 Boaz is willing to fulfill his duty as kinsman-redeemer **vv. 12–13** Plans to check with the closer relative but commits himself if the closer refuses **v. 14** Protects Ruth's honor by sending her away before the others awake **v. 15** Provides extra barley **v. 18** Naomi confirms Boaz will settle the matter quickly.	**v. 2** Boaz is kinsman — God's provision for Ruth and Naomi **v. 9** Spread your covering over your maid; kinsman-redeemer — picture of Jesus **v. 15** Boaz's provision for Ruth and Naomi is how God provided for them

Blessings — What, Who	Other Details
v. 10 Boaz blesses Ruth for not going after younger men.	

Chapter 4

Naomi's Character	Ruth's Character
v. 16 Became her grandchild's nurse	**v. 15** Called better than seven sons — the ultimate compliment in those times

Boaz's Character

vv. 1–4 Offers Naomi's land to the closer relative according to Scripture

vv. 5–6 Tells the other relative he must also take Ruth; the other relative is not able (would affect his inheritance according to the Law)

vv. 7–10 Legally acquires Naomi's land and Ruth to raise up the name of the deceased sons on his inheritance

v. 13 Loved Ruth and bore a son

God's Provision — What, How

vv. 1–10 Kinsman-redeemer; legal process for keeping land by families; set up in the Law => provided for Ruth and Naomi

v. 14 God provided a redeemer for Naomi.

vv. 17–22 Family line of David and ultimately Jesus

Blessings — What, Who

vv. 1–12 The witnesses bless Ruth and Boaz; fertility (like Rachel and Leah — the two who built the household of Israel), wealth, fame

vv. 14–15 The women bless Naomi after the birth of her grandchild. They bless the Lord for providing a redeemer. They bless the grandson that he will be famous, a restorer and a sustainer. They bless Ruth that she loves Naomi and is better than seven sons.

Other Details

v. 7 Exchange of a sandal confirms the legal deal

v. 17 Obed — the father of Jesse, the father of David

vv. 18–22 Generations — Perez to David

David's Story, Part 3—
Solomon Succeeds David

Stepping Stones
- ➤ Key Figure: David and Solomon
- ➤ Key Word: Disobedience
- ➤ Key Concept: Disobedience affected how Solomon participated in God's plan and promises.
- ➤ Key Bible Book: 1 Kings

186

Note: If this lesson is used, it should be presented in chronological order with the other lessons. Solomon's story should be taught after David's story. Find lesson handouts for participants, available online.

OVERVIEW
Lesson Objectives
- To see how our disobedience can affect how we participate in the plans and promises of God.
- God has made many important promises to David.
- David dies and his son, Solomon, succeeds him.
- Solomon starts out well, but then is disobedient to the Law.
- God punishes Israel for Solomon's disobedience, but is faithful to the promises He made to David.

Step 1   Begin the Lesson
- Pray—be sure to begin every lesson with prayer.
- Note that David has sons from several different wives.
- Briefly review the table below.
- Read 1 Kings 1:28–40.
  - David affirms that **Solomon** will be the son to succeed him to the throne.

KING DAVID'S WIVES AND SONS

WIFE	SCRIPTURES	SON(S)
1. Michal	1 Samuel 18:27 2 Samuel 3:3	None
2. Ahinoam	1 Samuel 25:43 2 Samuel 3:2 1 Chronicles 3:1	Amnon
3. Abigail	1 Samuel 27:3 1 Chronicles 3:1	Daniel (Kileab)
4. Maakah	2 Samuel 3:3 1 Chronicles 3:2	Absalom
5. Haggith	2 Samuel 3:4 1 Chronicles 3:2	Adonijah
6. Abital	2 Samuel 3:4 1 Chronicles 3:3	Shephatiah
7. Eglah	Judges 14:18 2 Samuel 3:5 1 Chronicles 3:3	Ithream
8. Bathsheba	1 Chronicles 3:5 2 Samuel 11:3	Shammua, Shobab, Nathan, and **Solomon**
Wives unknown	1 Chronicles 3:6	Ibhar, Elishua, Eliphelet, Nogah, Nepheg, Japhia, Elishama, Eliada, and Eliphelet

"These were the sons of David born to him in Hebron: The firstborn was Amnon the son of Ahinoam of Jezreel; the second, Daniel the son of Abigail of Carmel; the third, Absalom the son of Maakah daughter of Talmai king of Geshur; the fourth, Adonijah the son of Haggith; the fifth, Shephatiah the son of Abital; and the sixth, Ithream, by his wife Eglah. These six were born to David

in Hebron, where he reigned seven years and six months. David reigned in Jerusalem thirty-three years, and these were the children born to him there: Shammua, Shobab, Nathan, and Solomon. These four were by Bathsheba daughter of Ammiel. There were also Ibhar, Elishua, Eliphelet, Nogah, Nepheg, Japhia, Elishama, Eliada, and Eliphelet—nine in all. All these were the sons of David, besides his sons of his concubines. And Tamar was their sister."
—1 Chronicles 3:1–9

"Sons were born to David in Hebron: His firstborn was Amnon the son of Ahinoam of Jezreel; his second, Kileab, the son of Abigail the widow of Nabal of Carmel; the third, Absalom son of Maakah daughter of Talmai king of Geshur; the fourth, Adonijah the son of Haggith; the fifth, Shephatiah the son of Abital; and the sixth, Ithream the son of David's wife Eglah. These were born to David in Hebron." —2 Samuel 3:2–5

Step 2 Solomon Succeeds David to the Throne

- Read 1 Kings 2:1–4.
- David gives instructions to **Solomon** that tell him to do the following:
  - Be **strong**.
  - Observe what the LORD your God **requires**.
  - Walk in obedience to Him and keep His **decrees** and **commands**, His laws and regulations as written in the Law of Moses.
- After giving these instructions, David dies (1 Kings 2:10–12).

Step 3 Solomon Begins Well

- Read 1 Kings 3:5–15.
- The Lord appears to Solomon in a **dream** and says, "Ask for whatever you want me to give you."
- Solomon does not ask for **long life** or **wealth**, but instead asks for a **discerning** heart to govern the people and to distinguish between right and wrong (verse 9).
- The Lord is pleased that Solomon has asked for this, so what does the Lord give him? (See verses 11–14; also 4:30, 32.)
  - So God said to him, "Since you have asked for this and not for long life or wealth for yourself, nor have asked for the death of your enemies but for discernment in administering justice, I will do what you have asked. I will give you a wise and discerning heart, so that there will never have been anyone like you, nor will there ever be. Moreover, I will give you what you have not asked for—both riches and honor—so that in your lifetime you

will have no equal among kings. And if you walk in my ways and obey my statutes and commands as David your father did, I will give you a long life."

Step 4 Solomon Builds a Temple for the Lord

- Read 1 Kings 6:1–3.
  - "The temple that King Solomon built for the LORD was sixty cubits long, twenty wide and thirty high. The portico at the front of the main hall of the temple extended the width of the temple, that is twenty cubits, and projected ten cubits from the front of the temple."
    - In today's terms: 1 cubit = about 1.5 feet
    - That is, about 90 feet long, 30 feet wide, and 45 feet high or about 27 meters long, 9 meters wide, and 14 meters high.
- Read 1 Kings 6:38.
  - How long does it take Solomon to build the temple? **7 years**

Step 5 Solomon Disobeys

- Read 1 Kings 9:6–9.
  - The Lord gives Solomon a warning. What was it?
    - "But if you or your sons turn away from me and do not observe the commands and decrees I have given you and go off to serve other gods and worship them, then I will cut off Israel from the land I have given them and will reject this temple I have consecrated for my Name. Israel will then become a byword and an object of ridicule among all peoples. And though this temple is now imposing, all who pass by will be appalled and will scoff and say, 'Why has the LORD done such a thing to this land and to this temple?' People will answer, 'Because they have forsaken the LORD their God, who brought their fathers out of Egypt, and have embraced other gods, worshiping and serving them—that is why the LORD brought all this disaster on them.'"

- Read 1 Kings 11:1–6.
  - How does Solomon defy God's commands? What does he do that led him astray?
    - He loved many **foreign wives who worshipped other gods.**
    - He had **700** wives and **300** concubines.
    - God had originally commanded the Israelites not to intermarry with foreigners because they worshipped other gods. Deuteronomy 7:2–4
- Read 1 Kings 11:11–13.
  - What is the Lord's response to Solomon's disobedience?
    - So the LORD said to Solomon, "Since this is your attitude and you have not kept my covenant and my decrees, which I commanded you, I will

most certainly tear the kingdom away from you and give it to one of your subordinates. Nevertheless, for the sake of David your father, I will not do it during your lifetime. I will tear it out of the hand of your son. Yet I will not tear the whole kingdom from him, but will give him one tribe for the sake of David my servant and for the sake of Jerusalem, which I have chosen."

- We will also need to look at the original promise made to David in 2 Samuel 7:11–17.
  - In verse 16, The Lord said: "Your house and your kingdom will endure forever before me; your throne will be **established forever**."

Step 6   God Is Faithful to David

- Prophecies linking David to Jesus:
  - 1 Kings 11:13: "Yet I will not tear the whole kingdom from him, but will give him **one tribe** for the sake of David my servant and for the sake of Jerusalem, which I have chosen."
  - 1 Kings 11:36: "I will give **one tribe** to his son so that David my servant may always have a lamp before me in Jerusalem, the city where I chose to put my Name."

- Prophecy fulfilled:
  - 1 Kings 12:20: "When all the Israelites heard that Jeroboam had returned, they sent and called him to the assembly and made him king over all Israel. Only the tribe of **Judah** remained loyal to the house of David."
  - Luke 1:30–33: "But the angel said to her, 'Do not be afraid, Mary; you have found favor with God. You will be with child and give birth to a son, and you are to give him the name **Jesus**. He will be great and will be called the Son of the Most High. The Lord God will give him the throne of his father David, and he will reign over the house of Jacob forever; his kingdom will **never end**.'"
  - Revelation 5:5: "Then one of the elders said to me, 'Do not weep! See, the **lion** of the tribe of Judah, the Root of David, has triumphed. He is able to open the scroll and its seven seals.'"
- We will look at Matthew 1 for David and Solomon's lineage leading to Jesus.
  - How many generations are there from Abraham to Jesus?
  - **42**

Step 7   Summary

- God has been making promises all through the Old Testament.
- Some of these promises were conditional on the people's obedience as we saw from God's words to Solomon.

- Solomon disobeyed and the nation of Israel was torn in two, but God kept His promise to David that his throne would be established forever.
- We saw this promise fulfilled in Jesus Christ.

Step 8 Next Steps
- Introduce the next lesson you are planning to teach.
- Pray.

HANDOUT KEY: OPTIONAL LESSON 2—DAVID'S STORY, PART 3—SOLOMON SUCCEEDS DAVID

See King David's Wives and Sons on page 187.

Read 1 Kings 1:28–40.
David affirms that **Solomon** will be the son to succeed him to the throne.

Read 1 Kings 2:1–4.
- David gives instructions to **Solomon** that tell him to do the following:
  - Be **strong.**
  - Observe what the Lord your God **requires.**
  - Walk in obedience to Him and keep His **decrees** and **commands,** His laws and regulations as written in the Law of Moses.

After giving these instructions, David dies (1 Kings 2:10–12).

Read 1 Kings 3:5–15.
- The Lord appears to Solomon in a **dream** and says, "Ask for whatever you want me to give you."
- Solomon does not ask for **long life** or **wealth,** but instead asks for a **discerning** heart to govern the people and to distinguish between right and wrong (verse 9).
- The Lord is pleased that Solomon has asked for this, so what does the Lord give him (3:11–14; 4:30, 32)? **He would be the wisest man who ever lived, and God would also give him riches and honor.**

Read 1 Kings 6:1–3. Solomon begins to build a temple for the Lord.
"The temple that King Solomon built for the Lord was sixty cubits long, twenty wide and thirty high. The portico at the front of the main hall of the temple extended the width of the temple, that is twenty cubits, and projected ten cubits from the front of the temple."

In today's terms: 1 cubit = about 1. 5 feet. That is, about 90 feet long, 30 feet wide, and 45 feet high or about 27 meters long, 9 meters wide, and 14 meters high.

Read 1 Kings 6:38.

How long does it take Solomon to build the temple? **7 years**

Read 1 Kings 9:6–9.

The Lord gives Solomon a warning. What is it?

Read 1 Kings 11:1–6.

How does Solomon defy God's commands? What does he do that led him astray?

- He loved many **foreign wives who worshipped other gods**.
- He had **700** wives and **300** concubines.

God had originally commanded the Israelites not to intermarry with foreigners because they worshipped other gods. Deuteronomy 7:2–4

Read 1 Kings 11:11–13.

What is the Lord's response to Solomon's disobedience? We will also need to look at the original promise made to David in 2 Samuel 7:11–17.

- In verse 16, The Lord said: "Your house and your kingdom will endure forever before me; your throne will be **established forever**."

Prophecies linking David to Jesus:

- 1 Kings 11:13: "Yet I will not tear the whole kingdom from him, but will give him **one tribe** for the sake of David my servant and for the sake of Jerusalem, which I have chosen."
- Kings 11:36: "I will give **one tribe** to his son so that David my servant may always have a lamp before me in Jerusalem, the city where I chose to put my Name."

Prophecy fulfilled:

1 Kings 12:20: "When all the Israelites heard that Jeroboam had returned, they sent and called him to the assembly and made him king over all Israel. Only the tribe of **Judah** remained loyal to the house of David."

Luke 1:30–33: "But the angel said to her, 'Do not be afraid, Mary; you have found favor with God. You will be with child and give birth to a son, and you are to give him the name **Jesus**. He will be great and will be called the Son of the Most High. The Lord God will give him the throne of his father David, and he will reign over the house of Jacob forever; his kingdom will **never end**.'"

Revelation 5:5: "Then one of the elders said to me, 'Do not weep! See, the **lion** of the tribe of Judah, the Root of David, has triumphed. He is able to open the scroll and its seven seals.'"

We will look at Matthew 1 for David and Solomon's lineage leading to Jesus.

- How many generations are there from Abraham to Jesus? **42**

Jonah's Story

Stepping Stones
- ➢ Key Figure: Jonah
- ➢ Key Word: Repentance
- ➢ Key Concept: God calls ALL people to repentance, even disobedient prophets!
- ➢ Key Bible Book: Jonah

Note: If this lesson is used, it should be presented in chronological order with the other lessons. Jonah's story should be taught after David's story. See "Step 1—Before the Lesson" to assign drama parts before this lesson is taught. Find lesson handouts for participants, available online.

OVERVIEW
Lesson Objectives
- To see that God calls all people to repentance—even disobedient prophets!

Step 1 Before the Lesson
- The teacher should announce this lesson the class period before it is taught.
- Assign roles for the Jonah Drama. (See handout available online.)
- Give "actors" copies of the Jonah Drama and encourage them to read their parts ahead of time.
- Tell them they may just read (not memorize) the parts, but can also act them out as they read if they would like.
- Assign some students to be props. They can also make props if they want.

Step 2 Begin the Lesson
- Pray—be sure to begin every lesson with prayer.
- We have seen the people of God go from being just one man, Abraham, and his wife, Sarah, to a mighty nation ruled by a king.
- Sadly, the nation fell away from God, and God had to send prophets to call His people back to Himself.

- One of his prophets, Jonah, was called to a pagan nation in order to bring them to repentance. However, Jonah was a reluctant prophet because he considered this nation to be the enemy of his people.
- Here is his story and the lesson he learned from God.

Step 3   Introduction
- Point students to "The Bible Is Unique" handout.
  - What kind of book is Jonah? Prophecy
  - What group of prophecy books does it fall into? Minor Prophets
    - The first five books of prophecy are the Major Prophets and are the longer books of prophecy.
    - The rest of the books of prophecy are generally shorter books.
    - Major and Minor is not a designation of a book's importance, but of length. All the books of the prophets are important.
  - Look at the historical books on the handout.
    - First and 2 Samuel are the books that detail the beginning of the monarchy, the reigns of Saul and David.
    - First and 2 Kings are the history of the monarchy after David.
  - Solomon, David's son, followed David as king. After his reign, the nation split in two.
    - The Northern Kingdom was called Israel.
    - The Southern Kingdom was called Judah.
  - Both kingdoms began to fall away from the Lord, so He sent them prophets to call them back to Himself.
  - Jonah prophesied to the Northern Kingdom, Israel. 2 Kings 14:25
- Nineveh was the capital of Assyria.
  - It was the greatest city at the time because Assyria was the world power.
  - Assyria was the main enemy of Israel; eventually they would conquer Israel.
  - They practiced idolatry, worshipping a fish god and goddess.
- Tarshish
  - A city probably in Spain
  - 2,000 miles away from Israel where Jonah lived

Step 4   Performing the Drama
- "Actors" read and perform the drama.

Step 5   Process What You Experienced
- Ask performers:
  - Did you learn anything new as you prepared for your role?

- Ask all:
  - Did you see anything new as you read or watched the drama?
  - Do you have any questions? Anything you didn't understand?

Step 6   Additional Points to Make

- Nothing is ever wasted by God.
  - Jonah spent three days in a fish because of **disobedience**.
  - Then he shows up in Nineveh (where they worship fish gods) bleached and stinking like fish. Real attention-getter.
- God has **patience** with sinners — both Nineveh and His prophet, Jonah.
  - God initiates and pursues us — even when we run.
  - God is persistent even though Jonah is **running away**.
  - Just as with David, God brings Jonah's **sin** to him so he can **repent**.
  - Have them look up the following verses and read them aloud. What do these verses say about how God deals with sinners?
    - Ezekiel 33:11: **God takes no pleasure in the death of the wicked. He wants them to repent instead.**
    - 2 Peter 3:9, 15: **God is patient with us. He wants everyone to come to repentance. His patience means salvation.**
    - Romans 2:4: **God's kindness leads us to repentance.**
    - 1 Timothy 2:4: **God wants all men to be saved and to come to a knowledge of the truth.**
- Jonah eventually obeys God, but his heart is not in it. He is a **reluctant** servant, but God **uses** him anyway. This is God's **grace**.
- Why is Jonah displeased and angry?
  - He is **disconnected** from God.
  - Jonah is more concerned about a **plant** (his comfort) than a **city**.
  - Jonah doesn't like God's plan. He has his **own plan**—destruction of his enemies.
  - But God's plan prevails.
- Look at Jonah 4:2. Does this sound familiar?
  - It repeats Exodus 34:6–7 and Psalm 51:1.
  - Exodus 34:6–7 is God's proclamation of His name to Moses. It is His description of Himself, His character.
  - Jonah basically says that he knew God would **have mercy**.
  - In Psalm 51:1 David found **comfort** in God's character after he sinned with Bathsheba.
    - David was **tender** toward God and what God was doing in his life.
    - Jonah was disconnected from God and found no **comfort** in God's character.

- God is <u>sovereign</u> over all.
  - God sent the wind on the sea. Jonah 1:4
  - God provided:
    - A fish. Jonah 1:17
    - A vine. Jonah 4:6
    - A worm. Jonah 4:7
    - And the scorching east wind. Jonah 4:8
  - God has a <u>plan</u> and <u>purposes</u>.

Step 7 Summary
- In Jonah's story we see how God calls <u>all</u> people to repentance, even sometimes His prophets.
- God wanted to give the pagan city of Nineveh, capital city of the Assyrian nation, a chance to repent and avoid His judgment.
- God chose Jonah as his prophet to Nineveh, but Jonah was a reluctant prophet, mainly because he viewed the Assyrian people as enemies. He was also out of step with God and not tender to what God was doing.
- God worked in Jonah to bring him to repentance so he could do as God had commanded him.
- Even though Jonah was a reluctant prophet, the people of Nineveh repented when they heard God's message.

Optional
Lesson 3
196

Step 8 Next Steps
- Introduce the next lesson you are planning to teach.
- Pray.

HANDOUT KEY: OPTIONAL LESSON 3—JONAH'S STORY

- Jonah spent three days in a fish because of <u>disobedience</u>.
- God has <u>patience</u> with sinners. He is persistent even though Jonah is <u>running away</u>.
- Just as with David, God brings Jonah's <u>sin</u> to him so he can <u>repent</u>.

What do these verses say about how God deals with sinners?
- Ezekiel 33:11: <u>God takes no pleasure in the death of the wicked. He wants them to repent instead.</u>
- 2 Peter 3:9, 15: <u>God is patient with us. He wants everyone to come to repentance. His patience means salvation.</u>
- Romans 2:4: <u>God's kindness leads us to repentance.</u>
- 1 Timothy 2:4: <u>God wants all men to be saved and to come to a knowledge of the truth.</u>

- Jonah is a **reluctant** servant, but God **uses** him anyway. This is God's **grace**.

Why is Jonah displeased and angry?
- He is **disconnected** from God.
- Jonah is more concerned about a **plant** (his comfort) than a **city**.
- Jonah doesn't like God's plan. He has his **own plan**.

Compare Jonah 4:2 with Exodus 34:6–7 and Psalm 51:1.
- Jonah basically says that he knew God would **have mercy**.
- In Psalm 51:1, David found **comfort** in God's character after he sinned with Bathsheba.
- David was **tender** toward God and what God was doing in his life.
- Jonah was disconnected from God and found no **comfort** in God's character.

God is **sovereign** over all.
- He sent the wind on the sea.
- He provided:
  - A fish. Jonah 1:17
  - A vine. Jonah 4:6
  - A worm. Jonah 4:7
  - And the scorching east wind. Jonah 4:8

God has a **plan** and **purposes**.

In Jonah's story we see how God calls **all** people to repentance, even sometimes His prophets.

John 9—The Man Born Blind

Stepping Stones
> - Key Figure: The Man Born Blind
> - Key Word: Belief
> - Key Concept: Jesus healed. One believed and others rejected.
> - Key Scriptures: John 9

Note: This lesson can be taught in lieu of Lesson 13—Jesus—Miracles. Find lesson handouts for participants, available online.

OVERVIEW

Lesson Objectives
- To see how Jesus healed a man.
- To see how others reacted to this healing.

Step 1   Begin the Lesson
- Pray—be sure to begin every lesson with prayer.
- Today we will see a man come to faith in Jesus even when others rejected Him.
- Jesus performed miracles for many reasons. (Note: references listed are representative. There are many other examples that could be listed.)
  - In response to **a person's faith**
    - Healing the centurion's servant Matthew 8:5–13
  - To **teach**
    - "Don't you remember the five loaves for the 5,000?" Matthew 16:8–12
  - To **fulfill prophecy**
    - Jesus reads from Isaiah at the synagogue. "Today this Scripture is fulfilled in your hearing." Luke 4:16–21
    - Jesus references prophecies in Isaiah when He answers the messengers from John the Baptist. Luke 7:20–23
  - As a proof of **who He was**
    - Response to John the Baptist: Luke 7:20–23
  - Out of **compassion**
    - Raising the widow's son: Luke 7:12–15

198

- To <u>reveal</u> God's power
  - Heals man born blind: John 9:3
  - Jesus raises Lazarus from the dead: John 11:4
- People had different reactions to the miracles of Jesus. Some worshipped. Some saw their faith deepen. Others rejected Him or stirred up conflict.

Step 2   Prepare the Class
- Prepare the students to hear the story by defining some terms that may be unfamiliar.
  - Pharisees: These were some of the rulers of Israel during Jesus' time on earth. They were very strict adherents to the Law of Moses. They and the people thought of them as the best examples of what it meant to be faithful to God.
  - Sabbath: Saturday. This was God's holy day. After He finished creating, God rested on the seventh day and made it holy. Israel was expected to honor God on this day and to avoid all work. The Pharisees were especially sensitive to times when people broke the Sabbath.
  - Synagogue: These were established throughout Israel. It is where the Jewish people gathered for teaching and fellowship.

Step 3   Present the Story in John 9
- With feeling, read John 9 through for the students.
- Pass out the John 9 Drama Handout. (See handout available online.)
- Assign parts to the students.
- The teacher is the "director." At the beginning of each scene, bring up the actors in that scene. This will minimize the number of people at the front of the room. It also helps the class to see the action moving from scene to scene.
- Have the narrator announce each scene ("Scene 1" and so on).
- Have them read or act out the drama with feeling.

Step 4   Discuss the Story
- Why was the man blind?
  - Jesus said it was so that the <u>works of God</u> might be displayed. John 9:3
  - Why did the disciples think he was blind? <u>Sin</u> This was a common idea at that time. Bad things happened to people because someone sinned.
- How does Jesus identify Himself in verse 5? "I AM the light of the world."
- Notice the difference between how Jesus treats the man and how the Pharisees treat him.
  - Jesus <u>heals</u> the man.

- The Pharisees use him as a way **to accuse Jesus**. They throw him out of the synagogue.
- Jesus went back after the ordeal to comfort the man, and to identify Himself and give the man the chance to experience salvation by faith in Jesus.
- Why were the Pharisees so upset about this healing? Jesus did it on the **Sabbath**. They considered this as "work" on the Sabbath. They were unconcerned about the man. They only cared about adherence to the Law of Moses.
- To verify that a miracle had really happened, the Jews called for the man's parents to ask them if he had been born blind. What do you think about the parents' response?
  - They were **afraid**.
  - Why? The Pharisees were **powerful** people who could have them **thrown** out of the synagogue. Then they would have been cut off from God and His people.
- Notice what the man calls Jesus throughout the story (underlined in the drama handout available online). What is changing? His **understanding** of who Jesus is.

- Notice that the man stands up to the Jewish leaders (Pharisees) even **before** he fully understands who Jesus is. How was he able to do this?
  - He believed the **evidence**—I was blind, but now I see.
  - He doesn't have much other information and is not willing to speculate about things he doesn't understand. But no one can question the fact that he was once blind but now sees.
- When does the man fully believe in Jesus? **Not until the end** of the story when Jesus goes back to **talk** to him.
  - Notice that he stood up to the Jewish leaders even before he fully believed.
- When the man fully understood who Jesus was, he worshipped Him.
- Who should have believed, but did not? the **Jewish leaders** Why do you think this is?

Step 5   Summary

- Jesus healed the man born blind. Then the man was immediately challenged by the Pharisees, the Jewish leaders of the day.
- The man stood up to them even though his faith was not complete. He believed the evidence: "I was blind, but now I see."
- His faith became complete when he met Jesus the second time and Jesus identified Himself. Then he worshipped Jesus. John 9:35–38
- Jesus rebuked the Pharisees for their unbelief. They thought they were God's special people because they knew the Law, but they did not believe in the One the Law pointed to. So Jesus said they were guilty.

Step 6 Next Steps

- Introduce the next lesson you are planning to teach.
- Pray.

HANDOUT KEY: OPTIONAL LESSON 4—
JOHN 9—THE MAN BORN BLIND

Jesus performed miracles for many reasons including:

- In response to <u>a person's faith</u> Matthew 8:5–13
- To **teach** Matthew 16:8–12
- To **fulfill prophecy** Luke 4:16–21; 7:20–23
- As a proof of **who He was** Luke 7:20–23
- Out of **compassion** Luke 7:12–15
- To **reveal** God's power John 9:3; 11:4

Why was the man blind? So that the **works of God** might be displayed. John 9:3

Why did the disciples think he was blind? **Sin**

Optional
Lesson 4
201

Notice the difference between how Jesus treats the man and how the Pharisees treat him.

- Jesus **heals** the man.
- The Pharisees use him as a way **to accuse Jesus**.

Why were the Pharisees so upset about this healing? Jesus did it on the **Sabbath**.

What do you think about the parents' response? They were **afraid**.

Why? The Pharisees were **powerful** people who could have them **thrown** out of the synagogue.

Notice what the man calls Jesus throughout the story (underlined in the drama handout). What is changing? His **understanding** of who Jesus is

Notice that the man stands up to the Jewish leaders (Pharisees) even **before** he fully understands who Jesus is.

How was he able to do this? He believed the **evidence**.

When does the man fully believe in Jesus? **Not until the end** of the story when Jesus goes back to **talk** to him.

Who should have believed, but did not? the **Jewish leaders**

Why do you think this is?

The Crucifixion—*The Passion of the Christ* Film

Stepping Stones

> ➤ Key Figure: Jesus
> ➤ Key Word: Sacrifice
> ➤ Key Concept: Jesus gave His life to save sinners.
> ➤ Key Bible Books: The Gospel of Matthew

Option

- If you do not have time to show the entire film, *The Passion of the Christ*, you may instead find and show specific scenes in the film that correlate with Scripture passages noted in Matthew 26:17–75 and Matthew 27:11–52.
- You could also show the Crucifixion scenes from another movie, such as *The Jesus Film*, before teaching this lesson.
- Find lesson handouts for participants, available online.

OVERVIEW

Lesson Objectives

- To paint a visual picture of the sacrifice Jesus made for all sinners.

Step 1 Begin the Lesson

- Pray—be sure to begin every lesson with prayer.

Step 2 Review

- We have been getting to know Jesus.
- We looked at how He was born and how His birth fulfilled prophecies of the Messiah from the Old Testament.
- Then, we saw Jesus as He was introduced by His forerunner, John the Baptist, who said, "Behold the Lamb."
- Then we saw Him as He began His ministry, cleansing the temple and teaching a teacher, Nicodemus.
- In the last lesson, we talked about Jesus' miracles and healings.
- Now we will look at who He claimed to be.

Step 3   Before watching clips from *The Passion of the Christ*

- Explain to the group that we will be reading from the passages in Matthew 26:17–75 and Matthew 27:11–52 (aloud or silently depending on the amount of time available and the comfort level of the group) to compare and contrast with the movie *The Passion of the Christ.*

★ NOTE

We have found that many of the participants struggle with watching The Passion of the Christ *in its entirety without pausing for discussion. It is suggested that one passage of Scripture is read first and then a scene from the movie is shown. Discussion after each movie scene should be used to compare and contrast with the Scripture.*

- However, you will need to ensure that the scenes coincide with the following passages.

★ NOTE

The Passion of the Christ *is not in same order as we see in Scripture. Jesus' journey to the Cross is written chronologically, yet the movie flashes back and forth between scenes.*

- Scripturally, this is the order in which Jesus' journey to the Cross is depicted:
    - Matthew 26:17–30 . . . . . . Last Supper Speaking to His Disciples
    - Matthew 26:31–35 . . . . . . Jesus Predicts Peter's Denial
    - Matthew 26:36–46 . . . . . . Gethsemane
    - Matthew 26:47–56 . . . . . . Jesus Arrested
    - Matthew 26:57–75 . . . . . . Before the Sanhedrin & Peter Disowns Jesus
    - Matthew 27:11–26 . . . . . . Jesus Before Pilate
    - Matthew 27:27–31 . . . . . . The Soldiers Mock Jesus, Crown of Thorns
    - Matthew 27:32–52 . . . . . . The Crucifixion & The Death of Jesus
- Prior to reading the passages about the Last Supper, explain the significance of the Passover meal. Reference Exodus 12:1–9.
- Ask the class to note how Judas addresses Jesus compared with the other disciples (Matthew 26:22, 25).

Step 4   Watch specific scenes in *The Passion of the Christ* that correspond to the Scriptures.

- Section 1: Read Matthew 26:36–46
    - Scene 1 (0:00). . . . . Gethsemane
    - Scene 2 (3:20). . . . . Judas agrees to betray Jesus

- Scene 3 (8:22). . . . . .Jesus is tempted, crushes head of the serpent
- Additional references . . .Luke 22:36–49; Matthew 26:14–16; Genesis 3:15
- Section 2: Read Matthew 26:47–56
  - Scene 4 (9:14). . . . . .Jesus Arrested
    Peter cuts off Malchus's ear
  - Additional references . . .Luke 22:47–53; John 18:10–11
- Section 3: Read Matthew 26:57–75; 26:31–35
  - Scene 8 (23:12) . . . . .Before the Sanhedrin
  - Scene 9 (29:06) . . . . .Peter Disowns Jesus and Jesus Predicts It
  - Additional references . . .John 18:19–24; Luke 22:54–62; Matthew 26:69–75
- Section 4: Read Matthew 27:27–31; 27:11–26
  - Scene 17 (1:05:07) . . . . . .The Soldiers Mock Jesus, Crown of Thorns
  - Scene 19 (1:08:08) . . . . . .Jesus before Pilate
  - Additional reference . . . .Matthew 27:1–26
- Section 5: Read Matthew 26:17–30; 27:32–52
  - Scene 27–29
    (1:35:05–1:52:19). . . . . . . .The Last Supper, Scenes from the Crucifixion
  - Scene 30 (1:52:20) . . . . . .The Death of Jesus
  - Additional references . . .Exodus 12:1–9; Mark 14:22–25; Luke 22:17–20

Optional
Lesson
204

Step 5   Next Steps

- Pray.
- In the next lesson, we will begin to see what Christ did for us on the Cross.

OPTIONAL LESSON (IN LIEU OF LESSON 17)

The Resurrection—*The Passion of the Christ* Film

Stepping Stones

> ➤ Key Figure: Jesus
> ➤ Key Word: Redemption
> ➤ Key Concept: Jesus chose to give His life to save sinners.
> ➤ Key Bible Books: The Gospels of Matthew and John

OVERVIEW
Lesson Objectives
- To paint a visual picture of the choice Jesus made to sacrifice Himself for all sinners.

Step 1   Begin the Lesson
- Pray — be sure to begin every lesson with prayer.

Step 2   Review
- What disparities did you notice between the movie, *The Passion of the Christ* and Scripture?

Step 3   Discuss
- We recognize that Jesus suffered an unspeakable death, but why?

★ Application to Life

How far would *you* go to accomplish God's will?
What would you do if God asked you to die in the place of another?
What choice would you make?

Step 4   Before Watching Clips from *The Passion of the Christ*
- Ask someone in the group to read the passage from Matthew 26:47–56 aloud.
  - When Jesus was approached in the garden of Gethsemane to be arrested, Peter drew his sword trying to thwart the events that were about to happen.
- However, notice that Jesus reminds Peter that *it is by choice* that He sacrifices Himself (v. 53).

- Being the Son of God, Jesus could have, at any time, called on legions of angels to stop His arrest and crucifixion, but instead He chose to carry out God's will.
- It was with this choice that Jesus' disciples deserted Him and fled (v. 56).

★ Application to Life

Discuss the idea of choosing to follow God.

How would our friends and family react?

When we choose to follow God's will, we must be prepared to have our friends and loved ones not understand or support our choice. Some may even desert us. Jesus says in Matthew 7:13–14: "Enter through the narrow gate. For wide is the gate and broad is the road that leads to destruction, and many enter through it. But small is the gate and narrow the road that leads to life, and only few find it."

What are the costs for choosing to follow God?

Step 5   The Response to Jesus' Bold Statements and Choices
- Ask someone in the group to read the passage John 2:18–22 aloud.

DISCUSSION

Discuss John 2:18–22 and what it might mean in relation to the Crucifixion and Resurrection.

Ask the group to give their thoughts about what Jesus says in verse 19, "Destroy this temple and I will raise it again in three days."

Step 6 Watch the "It is finished" and the Resurrection scene in *The Passion of the Christ*
- Begin with specific clips to coincide with scenes from:
  - John 19:28–37   The Death of Jesus
  - Matthew 28:1–3   The Resurrection

Step 7   Next Steps
- Ask the group to share about any disparities they noted between the movie and Scripture.
- Ask them to reflect on what Jesus said in John 2:18–22 and apply it to the Crucifixion and Resurrection.

WorldCrafts™ artisan partner Graffiti 2 Works in the South Bronx of New York coaches adults in developing the physical, mental, emotional, social, and spiritual skills necessary to become the best he or she is capable of becoming. Program components include life skills, spirtual direction, mentoring, educational skills, career connections, and job incentive. Currently the group has four artisans who are taking classes with the goal of receiving their GED. These artisans range from 18 to 22 years old and have all lived in the South Bronx their entire life. Learning sewing skills and selling products not only provides them with a little money in their pockets, but it also builds their self-esteem and helps give them practical knowledge for the future.

WORLDCRAFTS℠

Committed. Holistic. Fair Trade.

WorldCrafts.org 1-800-968-7301

WorldCrafts is a division of WMU®.

RESOURCES FOR UPSIDE-DOWN LIVING!

To learn more about this series, visit NewHopePublishers.com.

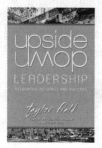

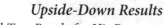

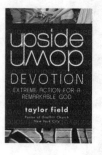